PRAISE FOR
TOWARD A HOLY ECOLOGY:
READING THE SONG OF SONGS
IN THE AGE OF CLIMATE CRISIS

"What happens when a rabbi with an expertise in biology reads the holiest and most sensuous book of the Bible? A fresh and arousing reading springs forth! Ellen Bernstein, founder of the first national Jewish environmental organization, offers an inspired ecological reading of the Song of Songs that will (re) kindle the reader's love affair with the earth. Her writing is as rich as the Song is evocative. Her interpretive insights reflect a deep engagement with the Song's poetic nuances. Cultivating an *eros* for creation, Rabbi Bernstein's interpretation is exactly what today's 'earth keepers' need for continuing the hard work of shalom-justice for the world. Call it 'Fifty Shades of Green.'"
—**William P. Brown,** *The Seven Pillars of Creation: The Bible, Science and the Ecology of Wonder*

"The lushness of Ellen Bernstein's eco-sensitive commentary on the Song of Songs is worthy of the original, which says a great deal about the ingenuity and power of her work. Bernstein reads the Song of Songs as a love song to and from the earth, and in so doing, uncovers truths in this long-beloved text that are essential, moving, and needed. She describes the 'archetypal intimacy between humans and nature' that evolves throughout the Song, as lovers co-mingle with the land and love itself burgeons as spring arrives. Bernstein's essential message, which she brilliantly derives from the text, is that 'beauty calls us to love the world.' This uplifting and enlivening book is an important and timely work—a wondrous gift to all who passionately love the earth, inviting us to find solace in the Bible's most erotic and egalitarian text." —**Rabbi Jill Hammer, PhD,** *The Jewish Book of Days: A Companion for All Seasons*

"*Toward a Holy Ecology* is a rich and illuminating commentary on the Song of Songs. Ellen Bernstein brings a unique voice that skillfully weaves scholarly and poetic insight. Her book is accessible for everyone interested in how this iconic text carries a deep ecological wisdom." —**Mary Evelyn Tucker, Co-director, Yale Forum on Religion and Ecology**

"Rabbi Ellen Bernstein's masterful commentary reveals the Song's profound vision of ecological wholeness and revives an embodied and earth-honoring tradition that is vitally needed today. This is an important, timely and beautiful book that deserves your attention." —**Rabbi Rami Shapiro,** *Judaism without Tribalism*

"Reading Ellen Bernstein's *Toward a Holy Ecology* is to partake in a garden of delights. She refreshes our reading of the Song by enlivening all of our senses. Her penetrating and compelling thought is expressed with eminently accessible and beautiful prose. Just as she highlights the importance of time and timing in the text itself, her commentary appears at just the right time to nurture a deepened ecological and embodied spirituality of which the world stands in urgent need." —**Rabbi Nancy Flam, Co-founder National Center for Jewish Healing, and The Institute for Jewish Spirituality**

"[O]ffering keen insight into both Jewish tradition and contemporary issues of environmental justice...the book will be accessible to lay readers and will challenge Jewish scholars with a well-grounded alternative view." —*Kirkus Reviews*

TOWARD A HOLY ECOLOGY

READING
THE SONG OF SONGS
IN THE
AGE OF CLIMATE CRISIS

RABBI ELLEN BERNSTEIN
FOREWORD BY BILL McKIBBEN

Monkfish Book Publishing Company
Rhinebeck, New York

Paperback ISBN 978-1-958972-19-9
eBook ISBN 978-1-958972-20-5

Library of Congress Cataloging-in-Publication Data

Names: Bernstein, Ellen, 1953- author. | McKibben, Bill, author.
Title: Toward a holy ecology : reading the Song of Songs in the age of
    climate crisis / Rabbi Ellen Bernstein, Bill McKibben.
Description: Rhinebeck, New York : Monkfish Book Publishing Company, [2024]
    | Includes bibliographical references.
Identifiers: LCCN 2023006978 (print) | LCCN 2023006979 (ebook) | ISBN
    9781958972199 (paperback) | ISBN 9781958972205 (ebook)
Subjects: LCSH: Nature--Biblical teaching. | Human ecology--Biblical
    teaching. | Bible. Song of Solomon--Criticism, interpretation, etc. |
    Nature--Religious aspects--Judaism. | Human ecology--Religious
    aspects--Judaism.
Classification: LCC BS1199.N34 B48 2024 (print) | LCC BS1199.N34 (ebook)
    | DDC 223/.906--dc23/eng/20230605
LC record available at https://lccn.loc.gov/2023006978
LC ebook record available at https://lccn.loc.gov/2023006979

Some of the ideas in this book first appeared in "The Ecotheology of the Song of
Songs" by Ellen Bernstein, in *The Oxford Handbook on the Bible and Ecology* edited
by Hilary Marlow and Mark Harris (New York: Oxford University Press, 2022)

Book and cover design by Colin Rolfe
Cover image in circle: "The Song of Songs II" (1957) by Marc Chagall

Monkfish Book Publishing Company
22 East Market Street, Suite 304
Rhinebeck, New York 12572
(845) 876-4861
monkfishpublishing.com

For you who love the earth and all her inhabitants

Integrity is wholeness
The greatest beauty is organic wholeness,
the wholeness of life and things,
the divine beauty of the universe.
Love that,
Not man apart from that.

—*Robinson Jeffers*

CONTENTS

FOREWORD

The Bible is the richest of all our books, filled with stories and images that manage to be both precise and open-ended. This means that as new challenges arise, those stories can be read again, in ways that shed new light on our particular moment. This new approach to the Song of Songs is a perfect example: read in the light of our present experience, with its almost overpowering ecological crises, it offers a wisdom that is intimate, penetrating, and utterly timely. Thank heaven that Ellen Bernstein has captured it so powerfully.

Let us not mistake what a revolutionary task this new kind of reading can be. For the most part, human literature has been about the conflicts between humans. That's where the action has been: wars, betrayals, jealousies, lusts, sacrifice. It's what the rabbis and the theologians—and the poets and playwrights and novelists—have concentrated on. Those intense human dramas have played out against a predictable backdrop of the natural world.

But in our time that backdrop is suddenly in motion—suddenly, in fact, it's the foreground. We need to work out how to conduct the relationship between people and the physical world, a relationship we've more or less taken for granted in the past. So we need to turn to our texts for advice on how to navigate it—not advice on how to generate clean energy (though it is nice to think that we're now turning from the fuels of hell to the fuels of the heavens) but on how to *be* in that world.

With a power matched only by God's soliloquy from the whirlwind at the end of the book of Job, the Song of Songs offers that vision. And where the tone of that soliloquy is mocking and harsh, here in the Song its power derives from its gentleness, creating, in Bernstein's words, "a profound sensual experience of the natural world. Over and over, it likens the lovers to the land and its inhabitants, asserting the indelible connection between humanity and earth. It reimagines the world as garden ecosystem, vibrant and whole and suffused with love. It pictures a land in which praise for the other, be it human or animal creature, plant or land, is continually on the lips of lovers."

As powerful as this reading is, of course, it only matters if we take it to heart—if we let it saturate us and move us to action. Because the world *can* be vibrant and whole, but that's not where it's headed at the moment. And if part of our job as humans is to feel that wholeness and to bear witness to it, another part of our job—laid out in the first page of the darned book—is to steward and nourish it. But we move to protect that which we first love. The Song of Songs is a call to that love, to a time capsule buried in the Bible for the moment we most need it. Which is now.

—Bill McKibben

MY JOURNEY WITH THE SONG OF SONGS

For several years, as a young adult, I worked as a river guide in northern California. In those halcyon days, when the long, rainy winter was over and the earth began to warm, my friends and I would drive to the foothills of the Sierras each year to greet the spring and begin to scout the rivers. The land was turning from parched brown to emerald-green, and luxurious mats of soft green moss and miner's lettuce, studded with tightly furled fiddleheads, stretched along the streambanks. The hills were covered with tiny, bright yellow buttercups and scarlet paintbrush. The music of goldfinches, bank swallows, and mourning doves filled the air.

In the evenings my friends and I would gather around a campfire and share the poetry of our favorite nature writers. I remember someone reading aloud a short passage from the Song of Songs. Though the Judaism of my childhood had never spoken to me, these words from the Bible opened my heart.

> Get up! My beloved, my beauty.
> Come away!

For now the winter is past,
the rain is over and gone.
The scarlet blossoms are shimmering in the land,
the time of the songbird has come,
the voice of the turtle is heard in our land.
The new figs have appeared,
the grape blossoms give off their sweet smell.
Get up! my beloved, my beauty; Come away!
(Song 2:10-13)

This passage perfectly captured my own experience of spring. Spring, as depicted in the Song, is vibrant and immediate—offering itself to be seen, smelled, eaten. Reading the Song, I could feel the spring well up in my blood; I longed to get up and run away with her. Whatever divinity I knew seemed to be bound up in this bodily experience of spring—of color, smell, and sound—of this torrent of energy and this romance with the earth. That the Song could articulate something I didn't have language for—that words from *my own* tradition could be meaningful—comforted and delighted me.

Charmed by the Song and the enigma of a turtle whose voice could be heard throughout the land, my partner and I named our river rafting company Turtle River.[1]

At that time, I had been studying biology, eager to learn as much as I could about the natural world. Still, I was often at a loss for language to express my awe at the innumerable intricate connections that enable life to flourish, and my concern for all the ways that we unwittingly inflict damage on the earth. Early on, I turned to writers like Annie Dillard, Lewis Thomas, and Wendell Berry to help me articulate my own sense of the beauty of the world. These nature writers encouraged me to see more clearly and deepen my own experience of nature. They dignified the life of the earth and gave voice to my inchoate feelings. There was something about the connection between the land and all of its creatures—including human creatures—that felt important.

After college, I taught high school biology. I wanted to share the wonder and beauty of the natural world with the young people who would be inheriting this earth. However, I found that the standard curriculum and textbooks bored my students, and they tuned out. I developed my own curriculum of great works of nature writing to try to capture their imagination. It worked: the students became hooked and their curiosity about the natural world blossomed. I realized then that stories, poetry, and literature can help shape our awareness of the environment and inspire a sense of responsibility for the earth.

Years later, I found myself wondering about the ecological dimensions of my own ancestral tradition, which I had long since abandoned. My instinct told me that any tradition that had lasted 3,000 years must have an ecological vision. It wasn't obvious to me then, but it was my early experience of that one fragment of the Song—its attention to the land and its creatures, and its vivid sense of the earth's energy rising in spring—that opened me up to consider the possibility of exploring Judaism. Faint childhood memories of verses from Jewish texts were also likely buried in my unconscious. I was rewarded generously when I began to take my search seriously. Once I gained a firm grasp of Hebrew and could read the texts in the original, I found ecological insight deeply embedded throughout the great Jewish books and particularly in the Hebrew Bible. I spent hours just plumbing the first chapter of Genesis, intrigued by its ecological depth.

For a few years, I tried unsuccessfully to find a Jewish

environmental organization that could support my interests and cultivate what felt like my calling. Ultimately, I realized that if I wanted to belong to such an organization, I would need to start it myself. So, with great trepidation, in 1988, I founded the first national Jewish environmental organization, *Shomrei Adamah*, Keepers of the Earth. The mission of the organization was to help illuminate the ecological dimensions of Judaism which had so long been overlooked. For the next decade, we researched and wrote articles, books, and curricula. We developed a foundation for thinking about Judaism from an ecological perspective.

In time, I turned my attention to the Song of Songs and was surprised by the centrality of the nature imagery throughout the entire book—not just in the few verses that I had first encountered as a young river guide. Gardens, vineyards, mountains, plants, and animals are ubiquitous throughout the text. A multiplicity of plants, animals and places are identified, and each creature is elevated and praised.[2] This profusion of varied life forms is a testament to the poet's reverence for nature. I realized that what I had intuited from my youthful days of reading the Song was true: The Song could be understood as a meditation on our relationship with nature, animated by love.

While the ancients and medievalists often interpreted the Song as an allegory of the relationship between God and the Israelites, many people in contemporary times have understood the Song simply as an erotic love story between a man and a woman. This is not surprising. The Song's lush sensuality and eroticism is so compelling that many of us gravitate toward the human story only. However, I contend that the Song is also a love story about the lovers and the land and its creatures; a story of the archetypical intimacy between human and nature. Eros is more encompassing that just a sexual relationship—it is life's endless desire to live, flourish and create.

Throughout the Song, the text is replete with figurative language, comparing the two lovers to many of the plant and animal species with whom they share the land. Yet a close reading reveals that it's not just that the lovers are like the other creatures—sometimes they seem to actually *become* the land and its creatures. Here, the woman is *like* a lily among the thorns—and here she *is* a garden locked. Simile gives way to metaphor, and metaphor binds together lover and landscape. "A lily is a lily is the woman's body is a man's lips is a field of desire."[3] An apple is an apple is the man's body, is a potion for the lovesick, is the place of conception and birth. The lovers comingle with each other as they do with the fecund land. The identity of the lovers is fused with an identification with the land.

Biologist Yehuda Feliks, whose career was dedicated to understanding the natural history of the plants and animals in the Hebrew Bible and who wrote his own commentary on the Song, posits that three love stories occur simultaneously in the Song.[4] One, as already mentioned, is the traditional allegory, for centuries considered the true meaning of the text for both Jews and Christians, in which the male character is understood as God and the female character as the people Israel. The second is the story of male and female lovers, which has become the more predominant reading in contemporary times. The third—Feliks's unique contribution—is the story of the love of a male and female gazelle.

Feliks suggests the male character morphs into his gazelle self when the woman calls his gazelle name. His suggestion echoes the ideas of the Netsilik people:

In the very earliest time
When both people and animal lived on earth
A person could become an animal if he wanted to
And an animal could become a human being.
Sometimes they were people
And sometimes animals
And there was no difference.
All spoke the same language.
That was the time when words were like magic.
The human mind had mysterious powers.[5]

I savored Feliks's commentary and felt that he was on to something that is too often disregarded in academic circles—a more embodied, intuitive and imaginative way of reading the text, an approach in which the senses are alive to all of nature. That a reputable professor of botany, zoology, and the Bible would see in the Song the transformation of a man into a gazelle, and that he could imagine the Song as the story of the gazelle's lifecycle, encouraged me on my own quest to illuminate the eco-theology of the Song. That quest has unfolded over two decades and has involved several projects that have culminated in this book.

Today we must engage whatever sources of wisdom we can to help nourish, strengthen and inspire us to meet the challenges of this ecological age. I believe the Song can both introduce its readers to deep ecological values and can help sustain these values. In a world threatened with ecological insecurity and a seemingly intractable divisiveness among groups, the Song bridges many divides, offering a vocabulary, a story, and a vision of interdependence and wholeness that all people can share.

PART ONE

THE IMPORTANCE OF THE SONG
FOR AN ECOLOGICAL AGE

About a decade ago, Gus Speth, former dean of Yale Law School famously said:

> I used to think the top global environmental problems were biodiversity loss, ecosystem collapse, and climate change. I thought that with thirty years of good science we could address these problems. But I was wrong. The top environmental problems are selfishness, greed, and apathy, and to deal with these we need a spiritual and cultural transformation, and we scientists don't know how to do that.[6]

It is the job of religion to help align us with our deepest held truths and values, and to reorient us to the path of justice and love. The environment, the climate, and the earth are not technological problems to be solved or mastered. They are complex living systems in which everything is connected to everything else. There is no single solution to the repair of our world. No one individual expert can figure it out.

The crisis we find ourselves in is a reflection our fundamental brokenness. We live in a culture that extols individualism and undervalues interdependence with each other and with the natural world. Our culture asserts that our happiness is a function of more money, more possessions and higher status, rather than a function of our health, our relationships, our communities, and our sense of purpose—all the things that money can't buy. These beliefs are embedded in our social, political, and educational systems. They are entrenched in a linear economy that takes resources from the earth and gives back contaminants and pollutants. They are so ingrained that we take them for granted. It is not just the whole earth, its plants and animals, and its systems and processes that suffer from our excesses. We human creatures have become estranged from nearly everything but the things we possess.

THE IMPORTANCE OF RELIGIOUS LITERATURE

Learning to love, appreciate and respect the earth and all its systems and inhabitants is not like learning a scientific theory or a historical fact. Our feelings and our values are not founded in rational thinking; rather they come from our direct experiences, our intuitions and the cultures that shape us. They need to be continually nurtured, taught and lived.

Jews and Christians have always turned to biblical literature to help nurture their values and keep them centered on paths of righteousness. The Song of Songs is among the most accessible of all biblical books: compelling, beautiful, provocative, and engaging to readers religious and secular, young and old. It is also the most deeply ecological text of the entire biblical canon.[7]

The Song sets the natural world before us with intensity and beauty and bids us to savor it with all of our senses, so that we may turn from the poem to see the natural world with renewed clarity and love. Especially for those of us who are Jews and Christians, who turn to Biblical poetry for liturgy and spiritual uplift, the Song's deep ecology may help heal us and show us what to attend to, and in doing so, teach us what to tend to.

In the course of its over 2,000-year history, the Song has been understood either allegorically or literally. It has been read as drama, and as cult literature. It has been sung in drinking halls. It is still performed at weddings and used as a guide in couples counseling. In Judaism, it is traditionally read every Passover and it is chanted in its entirety by observant Sephardic Jews every Friday evening.

The Song of Songs, we must remember, is also poetry. As such, it may be a particularly powerful way to communicate the subtle dimensions of ecology. Franz Kafka wrote that a literary work must be an ice-axe to break the frozen sea inside us. Kafka's frozen sea can be understood in the biblical idiom as a "hard heart" (In the Bible, Pharaoh epitomized hard-heartedness—he cared for little but his own exploits). Hard-heartedness separates us from each other and the world and undermines our ability to see and feel for the other. *Angaangaq Angakkorsuaq,* an Indigenous leader from Greenland better known as "Uncle," urges us to consider the melting glaciers of his homeland and implores us to melt the ice in our hearts so that we reconnect with one another to safeguard our lives and that of the life-giving earth.[8] Likewise, perhaps, the poet of the Song appeals to us to melt our hardened hearts so that we can truly come to connect with the other, be it human, animal, plant, or the land.

Today there is such urgency around our many earth crises, so much brokenness that we need a vision of wholeness and an ecological language that can help inspire, soothe, and reinvigorate us, and bring us together regardless of our various affiliations and orientations.

Perhaps the Song can offer a needed medicine to help revive and guide us.

ECOLOGICAL READINGS FOR ECOLOGICAL TIMES

I have long been partial to the word *ecology*, rather than the word *environment*, when speaking about our relationship with the natural world. *Ecology* is derived from the Greek words *oikos*, which refers to a house or dwelling place, and *logia*, which means the "study of." *Ecology* understands the earth as our home and is concerned with the relationships and processes that enable life on earth to flourish.

That ecology understands the earth as home implies an intimacy between us and the earth. The indissoluble connection between people and the earth is inscribed in the Hebrew language: *Adam*, the Hebrew word for "human" is nested inside of the word *adamah*, the Hebrew word for "earth." That few of us live with this consciousness is a fundamental problem of our times. We can see but can't fully know tree, rock, river, winged creature, or the climate until we learn to connect to the body of the earth through our animal bodies.

The ecological dimensions of a text are often more subtle and nuanced than the explicit moral messages that many associate with environmentalism. While the term "ecology" recognizes that people are embedded in a larger earthly system, the more popular term "environment" refers to our surroundings and implies a separation between us and that which is outside of us; it feels cold and abstract to me. Prescriptions for environmental actions should not be considered the primary standard for judging the ecological nature of a text. We need to consider how the text creates a world, not just what the author tells us to do or not to do.[9]

Sadly, much of today's environmentalist rhetoric can reduce the textures, the stories, the aliveness of the natural world into a simplistic environmental equation. It can unintentionally come across as preachy or self-righteous and can alienate as much as motivate. It can increase feelings of depression and bereavement that many of us already experience as we consider the future of life on earth. Indeed, climate anxiety has become a bona fide psychological condition. On the other hand, ecological literature has the potential to help heal us and guide our way home.

WHO IS THIS COMMENTARY FOR?

This commentary seeks to reach anyone interested in the intersection of spirituality and ecology. The Song never speaks the name for the divine, yet it is a deeply spiritual work that can reach many people who are interested in matters of the sacred but prefer to steer clear of God language. The Song's encounter with the divine is radically different than the other books of the Bible and is especially powerful for this ecological age. In both the Jewish and Christian worlds, where many people are disengaging from religion altogether, the Song—with its universal themes of love, justice and the integrity of nature—may help open the door to the possibilities that religion has to offer.

This commentary also seeks to address a more secular audience of environmentalists, academics and students in the fields of environmental ethics, the environmental humanities and religion and ecology. The Song of Songs is one of the oldest examples of ecological thinking and should take its rightful place in the canon of environmental literature.

However, even as this spiritual-environmental crisis intensifies, the division between the humanities and sciences in academia continues to cut ever deeper. Within the environmental humanities, biblical religion is often overlooked or dismissed. In geography and environmental studies courses, when the relationship of human to nature is discussed in light of religious traditions, it is not uncommon for all of biblical literature to be reduced to one passage: Genesis 1:28, which gives humanity "dominion" over the earth and its creatures. In these courses, "dominion" is invariably understood as "domination"—a jaundiced and simplistic reading of the text, yet one that has become popular and prevalent in academia, ever since the publication in 1967 of historian Lynn White's *Science* magazine article, "The Historical Roots of the Ecologic Crisis."[10] In many circles, the Bible is seen as the enemy of the environment. At a time when we are all being called to work together on behalf of the earth, when young people are hungry for meaning and direction, we must broaden the lens to offer a range of wisdom from varied traditions to help all of us navigate these difficult times.

"WHOLINESS": THE SONG'S MESSAGE FOR TODAY

Two thousand years ago, the renowned Rabbi Akiva called the Song of Songs the "holy of holies."[11] Through the ages people have wondered what Akiva meant by this, since the Song never refers to the divine, nor does it speak a conventional religious language.

If the holy one is not explicitly named in the *Song*, then what makes the Song holy? How else might godliness be conveyed? These are the questions that this commentary considers. In Judaism we can know God's work as evidenced by the creatures and processes of the natural world. The very first place God is revealed in the Bible is in a garden, and the very first conception of the divine is as creator, architect of the habitats, dreamer of the plants and animals, at home strolling in the garden of the earth.

The Song, too, is a garden ecosystem—lush and alive with green growing things. Some have suggested that the garden of the Song is a return to the mythical Garden of Eden, when the world was whole and seemingly inviolable. In that world, each creature had a purpose and a place, and all were bound together in an interconnected web. Indeed, in the beginning of the biblical creation story, God saw every creature as "good"—inherently valuable—and saw the entire interconnected web of creatures as "very good"—an integrated whole.[12] However, by the end of the creation story, the cosmic web had unraveled: the idyllic Eden suffered a three-way fracture: a fracture between man and woman, between people and the land and its creatures, and between people and God.[13] What began in wholeness ended in disintegration and alienation.

In this commentary, I maintain that the Song of Songs redeems the wholeness of the paradisial garden, and in so doing restores the presence of the holy. I call this divine ecological unity "wholiness." In the Song, the once broken relationship between man and woman is repaired through the mutual love and just relations of the lovers. The relationship between people and creatures is repaired through the characters' identification with the animals and plants of the land. Finally, the relationship between people and the Creator is repaired as reciprocity, balance, and wholeness are restored.

PART TWO

READING THE SONG ECOLOGICALLY

I swear the earth shall surely be complete
to him or her who shall be complete.
The earth remains jagged and broken
only to him or her who remains jagged and broken.

—*Walt Whitman*

Many people do not recognize the Song's ecology because the Song speaks its own ecological language. It is the intention of this commentary to help illuminate that language.

The ancient rabbis said, "Turn It, Turn it, because everything is in it." "Turning" a text means placing it in new contexts and conversations in order to illuminate new possibilities and understandings. Just as juxtaposing one color with another can change the way we perceive the color and can bring out new depths and tonal qualities, so placing a text in new contexts can illuminate new meanings of the text.

As we have discussed, "ecology" literally means the "study of the house." Spiritually speaking, the entire natural world is "God's house." In these essays, I try to tease out the kinds of relationships and values that contribute to the health, whole-ness, and resilience of the "house." Each essay suggests a different context for considering the interconnections between the characters of the Song and the natural world, and the ways in which the Song can speak to our ecological age.

The first essay, "Ecological Identity," explores the affinity between the couple and the natural world and their identification with its creatures and places. The second essay, "Cycles of Time," is interested in the characters' relationship to the cosmic rhythms. The third essay, "Beauty," reflects on the couple's experience of nature's beauty and contemplates beauty's ability to help us overcome our separation from nature. The fourth essay, "Justice," illustrates how a balanced, reciprocal relationship between male and female forms the bedrock for the healthy relationships of the entire living world. The final essay, "Wholiness," considers the Song's vision of ecological wholeness as an expression of the oneness and holiness of God.[14]

ECOLOGICAL IDENTITY

Being a responsible citizen of the earth requires us to rec-ognize the earth's aliveness, and to live in ways that honor this aliveness. It means expanding our identity beyond our particular affiliations or groups to include the whole natural world. The Song naturally communicates this expanded sense of identity. The two central characters are at home in the nat-ural world and identify with the various creatures and spaces within it. Unlike much of Western literature, where the land and its creatures merely serve as a backdrop to the human story (that is, when they are present at all), the Song pulsates with the aliveness of nature. Plants and animals occupy more of the foreground of the text. Each creature and each place hold meaning. As the lovers direct their loving admiration to each other, they are, at the same time, attending to the whole living world around them.

The lovers' language reveals their identification with the land and its creatures. The Song employs rich metaphors and similes to connect the lovers—and us, the readers—to the natural world. As the naturalist Alexander Von Humboldt knew, "we can only truly understand nature by using our imagination."[15] The figurative language of the Song invites us to imagine ourselves as being one with the land. Over and over, in more than half of the verses, the lovers liken them-selves and each other to the plants, animals, minerals, habi-tats, cities, and monuments of the land of Israel.

The lovers refer to themselves and each other as the particular flowers of the land. The female character, the *ra'yah*, calls herself a lily of Sharon; her belly is ringed with lilies. The lips of the male, the *dod*, are lilies, and he browses among the ra'yah's lilies. They also compare themselves and each other to fruits. He is like an apple tree. She smells like apples, and she craves apples. He is conceived under an apple tree, and she arouses him under an apple tree.[16] And they identify with the animals. He is called a gazelle and so is she—her breasts are like twin fawns of a gazelle.[17] The *dod*'s pet name for his love, *ra'yah*, means friend yet is similar to the word for shepherd. The *ra'yah* is a shepherdess, keeper of the sheep, and she is friend—her affections lie with the land and its plants and animals, just as they do with her lover.

The boundary between human and nature in the Song is porous, and the identity of the lovers flows back and forth seamlessly from body to land (creature) to body. The lovers identify so fully with the flora and fauna of their world that it is not always clear whether the poet is referring to the lovers or the other beings of the land. Literal translations can help illuminate the ambiguities of the text. When the *ra'yah* says,

> Here! He is coming:
> leaping over mountains,
> sprinting over hills. (Song 2:8)

we do not know if "he" refers to man or gazelle. The Hebrew *zeh* (literally, "this") is ambiguous; it can refer to a person, animal or thing. This vagueness arouses our curiosity: does the lover embody the attributes of the gazelle—agility, symmetry, speed? Or might the lover become a gazelle as the Israeli botanist Yehuda Feliks wonders? Might the lover transform from human to animal and back?[18] Since so much of the Song takes place in the lovers' dreams and imagination, there are countless possibilities.

More than just the individual flora and fauna, the couple identifies with the entire land of Israel. The Song's geography encompasses the whole land stretching north to Lebanon, south to Ein Gedi and the spice gardens, east to Heshbon and west to Mt. Carmel. Scholars have suggested that thirty-four distinct mountains, regions, cities and landscapes are specified, including Seir, Hermon, Tirtzah, Jerusalem, Lebanon, Armana, Hebron, the spice mountains, and the nut grove.[19] Six of Israel's seven species, signifying the land, are named: fig, grape, wheat, pomegranate, date, and oil.[20] The "honey and milk" under the ra'yah's tongue in Song 4:11 alludes to the biblical epithet for Israel as the "land of milk and honey."[21] With so many indicators of the land, it's undeniable that the land is key to understanding the meaning of the Song.

It's not just that the lovers appreciate and value the land and its creatures. Rather, the Song reads the land and its creatures onto the lovers' bodies. They *are* the land. As the ra'yah and dod admire the details of each other's anatomy, it is as if they are traversing the entire land of Israel. Traveling imaginatively either southward from head to toe, or north from foot to head, they praise the flora, fauna, and the precious minerals of the land.[22]

Gardens and vineyards are the most luxurious and evocative places of the Song, and it is here that the lovers feel most at home. Gardens are the rendezvous sites for the lovers; the oases where love is kindled and nurtured. However, it's often unclear—it seems intentionally so—whether the garden refers to a real garden or to the garden of the woman's body.

In the mid-section of the poem, the lovers' relationship intensifies in a garden (or in *her* garden), as the *dod* pines:

> A locked garden is my sister, my bride,
> a locked well, a sealed spring.
> Your branches are an orchard of pomegranates
> with the choicest fruits (4:12-13a)

Here, is the author referring to an actual garden and an actual tree or to the woman as garden and tree? As the *dod* reaches up into the branches, does he imagine her body as a tree or a tree as her body? In the Song, a garden is not just a metaphor. She is not *like* a garden; she *is* a garden spring (4:13-15). In addition to being a poetic device, the metaphor reveals the interconnection of woman, garden, fountain, and tree. Michael Fishbane suggests, "The depths of her soul are nurtured by the depths of the earth."[23] She, the woman-tree, arises from the earth, watering the garden and sustaining every fragrant tree and plant.

In the *dod*'s final praise poem of the *ra'yah*, images of diverse trees morph into one single, bountiful life-giving tree.

> Your stature is like a palm tree
> and your breasts like clusters.
> I said, Let me climb into that palm tree,
> let me grasp its branches.
> May your breasts be like grape clusters,
> and the scent of your breath like apples. (7:8-9)

Overcome with the *ra'yah*'s beauty, the *dod* stretches his mind to find language to capture his experience of her. He piles up images of all the trees, fruits, and fragrances he can think of.

She is an apple-scented palm tree with grape clusters, and he climbs up into her, clutching her life-giving fruits. With changing pronouns and the references to a tree and its various features, one wonders if the subject is the *ra'yah* or the tree. Perhaps it is both; perhaps that is the point.

Indeed, in the Song, the lovers are inexorably bound to each other and the land; its milk and honey; its pomegranates and figs; its cities, Jerusalem and Tirtzah; its tower of Lebanon. Attuned to the subtleties of the land, they are drawn to the place of the mother, the place where life began—to celebrate their courtship. They return to the "house of her who bore me," to "the apple tree," to conceive new life.[24] Like salmon and gazelle who return to their familial breeding grounds to give birth, the couple shows a kind of fidelity to place.

The Song teaches that ecological identity is an elemental aspect of human nature. Yet, in our insular, mechanized, and frenzied technological lives, we are cutting ourselves off from our roots, and our natural ecological sensibility is withering. In contemporary times, "identity" carries an entirely different meaning than it did even a generation ago. Today, many people regard identity as a function of a particular group to which they belong—be it ethnic, racial, religious, or political, gender, or sexual. Yet, when we gravitate too much toward a particular identity, we risk losing sight of our universality and our interdependence with all beings. And this is deeply concerning because, now more than ever, all of the earth's creature are afflicted by the ecological instability that climate change has wrought. The first step toward ecological repair is to love and identify with the natural world. Our lives—and the lives of all those who come after us—depend upon it.

CYCLES OF TIME

From an early age we assume that time moves in a linear fashion. We think of life as a steady progression of events, and we approach time as a resource to use, master, and control. Seventy years ago, in his searing critique of modern life, the renowned Rabbi Abraham Joshua Heschel wrote that we use time to conquer space.[25] We aspire to do more, produce more, and achieve more in less time. Speed has become a primary value of modernity. We rush to buy the fastest new electronic device to keep up with the dizzying pace of modern life.

The *Song* situates us in a different kind of time. With its long descriptive passages and infrequent use of active verbs, time slows down and spreads out. Time is rhythmic and cyclical, not just linear. There is a season for everything.

All beings—including human ones—whether consciously or not, are affected by the seasons of the earth as it travels around the sun. We are often so preoccupied that we don't pay attention to these rhythms, but they shape our lives as they do all creatures. In spring, emerald shoots appear out of the naked earth and the land turns green. Plants bud, then flower. In the summer, they fruit. In the fall, the plants drop their leaves and the seeds of their fruits travel through the air or along the digestive tracts or on the backs of animals to root in the soil—sometimes to an entirely new place. In wintertime, plant life goes dormant. With the longer days and the warmth of spring, the earth once again sprouts green, and the cycle begins anew. Animals too live by the seasonal cycles: they mate, conceive, gestate, grow, and hibernate according to the seasonal round.

The lovers of the Song also abide by these cosmic rhythms. Feliks suggests that the Song chronicles the cycles or nature as it chronicles the cycle of love.[26] The Song opens at the end of summer, as evidenced by the *ra'yah*'s sun-scorched skin (1:5-6). In the next scene, the long, cold, winter rains are over and past (2:11). Spring is coming. The turtle doves arrive home from their migrations, filling the air with song. The first flowers burst into bloom, painting a scarlet landscape, and the green figs appear.

Animated and emboldened by the welling up of the energy of early spring, the *dod* knocks on the door of the ra'yah, rousing her from her winter slumber as if to entice her on the spring migration (2:9,13).[27]

The couple's love blossoms as they encounter each other through the flowering season. With spring's longer, warmer days, love unfolds as the tight buds unfurl into blooms. The ra'yah, eager for love's consummation, goes to the nut garden to see if the vines have blossomed and the pomegranates have flowered, to see if the time has arrived for love's fulfillment (6:11). But the fruits are not ready; it is not yet time.

The lovers wait. Together they visit the garden again and this time they find ripe fruits hanging heavy on the branches and the scent of the *duda'im*, the love fruit or mandrake, hanging heavy in the air (7:12-14).[28] Now is the time. In these warm, blissful days on the cusp of summer, the lovers gather in the fruits of their well-seasoned love, and fully reveal themselves to each other (7:13-14).

The timing of the lovers' revelation is significant from a Jewish perspective. According to Feliks, it is at *Shavuot*, the season of revelation, that the lovers consummate their love. Shavuot is the time in the Jewish calendar when God reveals God's love to the people by giving them the Torah. Shavuot is also the time that the fruit of the wheat is "revealed;" ready to be harvested after a precarious forty-nine-day growing season.[29] Finally, Shavuot is the time that the Israelites would reveal their own love, offering two loaves of bread up to God in recognition of the blessings of Torah and wheat.

In the Song, at the moment when the lovers reveal themselves to each other, sharing both the fruits of their bodies and the fruits the *ra'yah* has gathered, the story of the lovers, the story of nature and the story of Israel all coincide (7:12-14).

In the Song, love, like nature, has its own innate rhythm. Love ripens in its own time like the fruits in the garden, and like the gazelles who find love in the season of their receptivity. Love can't be forced; each lover must be ready for it. Until the moment that love is ripe, one seeks in vain to find it. In the Song, the *ra'yah*'s thrice repeated refrain, "Don't wake; don't excite love till it pleases," is a persistent reminder that love will unfold in its own time (2:7, 3:5, 8:4).

Some interpreters of the Song, especially those who approach the Song as an expression of free love and read the text as a series of sexual encounters, ignore the centrality of timing in the text. They do not perceive the Song as a testament to the significance of natural rhythms, and the maturation of love. Were the Song simply a celebration of sexual freedom as some have suggested, one would think it would be the daughters of Jerusalem—representing a more conventional view—who would insist that the *ra'yah* exercise caution in relationship with her *dod*. Here, however, it is the *ra'yah* who beseeches or perhaps reprimands the daughters of Jerusalem, "Do not awake or arouse love until it pleases." Love needs protection from harmful outside influences; it will unfold organically in its own time. Nothing must interfere with love's gestation.

The centrality of timing in the Song is also evident as each lover seems to follow their own individual wavelike trajectory: their own biorhythms. For each, love ebbs and flows just like the tides and the daylight and the breath. First one lover, then the other, reaches out to connect, but misses. The dod approaches the *ra'yah* but then hides behind a wall. The *ra'yah* pursues the *dod* into the streets, but he slips away into the night (3.2). The *dod* knocks at her door, but the *ra'yah* hesitates, and he leaves without a word (5:2-6). Each lover is on their own journey—turning toward and turning away— just as the earth rotates, turning toward and away from the sun.

The Song teaches that love cannot be willed or determined. Love, like the whole of nature, seems to be tuned to the rhythms of the cosmos. When we become more conscious nature's cycles, we can learn to live more harmoniously and respectfully with the earth. We can come to better understand our own cycles, accept our limits, and respond more fluidly to life's uncertainties.

BEAUTY

How can we motivate ourselves and our communities to care for the natural world when its countless gifts continually escape our notice? Simply paying attention to the beauty of the natural world can be the first step on the beginner's path. This may seem so patently obvious as to be trivial. But, as Sandra Lubarsky, author and president of Flagstaff College argues, we have lost touch with the value of beauty just as we have lost touch with the value of the living natural world. She writes,

> Though it is not generally noted in the litany of loss that includes fresh water, soils, rain forests, coral reefs, and innumerable species, beauty is very much a casualty of ecosystem destruction and the increase of human demands on the planet. Its absence is conspicuous: the decapitation of mountains in Appalachia and the subsequent dumping of fill material—soil, trees, plants, rocks— into valleys and streams; the abraded landscape of the Canadian tar sands, denuded of boreal forests; ... ghost forests along the Eastern US coast, salt-killed by rising sea levels. These ecological disasters are also aesthetic disasters. We rarely note the loss of beauty, not because it isn't real or because we

> aren't disturbed by it, but because we have
> been trained not to take beauty's value into
> account.[30]

When the fight for the environment becomes too abstract and calculated, it's easy for people to disengage or retreat. The experience of beauty, on the other hand, is direct and immediate. Its impact may be deeply felt without being understood. It can wake us up, energize us and motivate us to act on behalf of the earth.

The value of beauty is fundamental to the meaning of the Song. The Hebrew word for "beauty," *yafah*, appears more in the Song than anywhere else in the Bible—approximately one-third of all the biblical occurrences of *yafah* show up in the Song.[31] The *ra'yah* is the embodiment of beauty.[32] She is repeatedly called "beautiful" by her beloved. He is also called beautiful by her, though not as often (1:16). The central animal in the Song is a gazelle; its Hebrew name, *tzvi*, can also mean "beauty." Many other terms expand the Song's repertoire of beauty: *naveh*/pleasant, *tov*/good, *aimah*/awe-inspiring, *nayim*/delightful, *matok*/sweet, and *erev*/pleasing.

In four long passages interspersed throughout the Song, each lover paints an alluring portrait of the other's beauty.[33] Each begins and ends their poem with the breathless exclamation, "Oh, you are beautiful," or something similar. In between, they testify to the lover's beauty with a litany of metaphors: "You are beautiful... Your eyes are like doves... Your hair like a flock of goats... Your teeth, like a flock of sheep... Your temples like pomegranates... Your breasts like two fawns"(4:1-5). These metaphors require an imaginative leap, especially for those of us who may live more insular lives detached from the natural world. But the point is that the lovers turn to the natural world over and over, reaching for language—for the colors, shapes, scents, tastes, and feelings—to articulate their experience. The only words the lovers can find to capture the loveliness of one another come from the creatures of the land with whom they live in kinship.

The *ra'yah* and the *dod* first apprehend beauty in the land. They only know what beauty is because they have seen the gazelles in flight and the sheep on the mountainside, and because they have been overwhelmed by the sight of Jerusalem and Tirtzah. The lovers' experience of the beauty of the land enables them to recognize the fullness of beauty in each other. Her beautiful body *is* the land, and it is full of Israel's creatures.[34]

Beauty in the Song is clearly not the idealized, symmetrical, or abstract beauty of the Greeks, although occasional references to symmetry occur as in the images of twin gazelles and twin teeth (4:2, 4:5 6:6,7:4). The poet presents impressionistic images rather than a definitive likeness. Beauty in the Song is visual, aromatic and tactile; it is textured and complex—a synesthetic experience. Beauty is a function of the abundance of the natural world.[35] It is a function of aliveness. Beauty only becomes intelligible through the Song's figurative language, which collapses the distance between the lovers and the land they inhabit. What beauty actually looks like in the Song is a luxurious land, alive with sheep grazing on hillsides, gazelles bounding through mountains, and trees laden with fruit.

For decades, many environmentalists rejected the idea that the beauty of nature could be a significant motivator to encourage people to care and act for the preservation of the earth and its inhabitants. Aesthetic appreciation of nature, especially that which is grounded in the picturesque, has been criticized as "anthropocentric, scenery-obsessed, trivial, subjective, and/or morally vacuous."[36] Beauty in our culture is so often associated with narrowly constructed standards for women's appearance or with products developed by savvy marketers in the clothing and cosmetics industries, that the word itself has sadly become tainted.

In the Song the poet turns to the language of beauty to convey a sense of wonder. Beauty excites the senses, stirs the imagination, and quickens the heart. The lovers forget themselves as they lavish praise upon and celebrate the goodness of each other and the whole natural world. In the face of overwhelming beauty, the self dissolves. Beauty can help overcome the "dualistic I" at the core of our separation from nature.[37]

Hurrying about, focused on the daily tasks before us, we often overlook the beauty of the living world in our midst. We need to slow down long enough so that our senses can attune to the verdant world around us. The Song teaches that if we are open to it, beauty can stop us in our tracks; it can draw us into a state of contemplation—or, in Rabbi A.J. Heschel's words, a state of "radical amazement." It can arouse our curiosity, our appreciation, and our humility.

The experience of beauty can strengthen our inner resources and our resolve to act on behalf of that which we love. Beauty calls us to love the world—and act for the sake of the whole earth. Beauty and love are of a piece, entwined together. Wendell Berry has argued that it is not enough to just *value* the natural world. If we want to save it, we must also *love* it, since love implies a responsibility, and therefore a giving back to that which we love.

The language of the beauty of nature can be especially important in communicating an environmental message to diverse audiences. It provides a vocabulary that can speak across political, ideological, and ethnic divides to capture something of the awe of the living world. Beauty can knit us together under the banner of love and encourage us to work to insure the health and resiliency of the earth.

JUSTICE

The same worldview and value system that leads to the exploitation of the earth also leads to the exploitation of women and marginalized groups. A healthy earth, like a just society, requires the balancing of male and female energies. The Song models such a balance.

Womanhood

The Song recovers the feminine and the centrality of the mother. Notably the female, the *ra'yah*, is the central character of the Song. She speaks the first word and the last, initiates much of the action and is continuously praised. She is independent and strong, a shepherdess with a well-developed identity. She is most at home in the natural world; happiest in the embrace of the green gardens and among the apple trees. Her life is a celebration of the earth, the ultimate mother.

The Song's appreciation of womanhood is heightened by the repeated references to a mother, with no mention of a father. Even Solomon, the king, receives his life-giving blessing from his mother who crowns him. And the *ra'yah*'s brothers are referred to only in terms of the mother—they are her "mother's sons."

The "mother's house" in the Song is a mythic and evocative place, associated with apple trees—the Song's signature fruit-bearing tree. The couple's return to the "mother's house" is imperative. It is as if they are magnetically drawn there to partake of the blessing of the feminine source of life. Like their mothers before them, they return to the apple tree to inaugurate new life. While the ra'yah is not yet a mother, she identifies with her own life-giving mother and the mother earth.

The Song is an ode to the generative nature of the feminine—both the land and the body. The blurring of boundaries between woman and land, and woman and tree, intensify the sense that the woman, like the land, is generative. The image of woman as a garden watered by fountains and streams is especially evocative of her life-giving nature. The many fruits of the Song—date and grape clusters, seed-filled pomegranates, and heaps of wheat—reverberate throughout the Song, emphasizing the fecundity of woman and fecundity of land.

Reciprocity

In the Song, the ra'yah and dod live in a dynamic reciprocity. Each is whole and complete. Neither dominates the other. The ra'yah desires the dod, as he desires her.[38] The dod's primary activity is appreciation of the ra'yah (who also stands for the natural world). Each lover regards the other as subject, not object: in Martin Buber's terminology, as "thou," not "it." The ra'yah's declaration, "I am my beloved's, and my beloved is mine" captures this feeling of mutualism.[39] The dialogical nature of their relationship, unlike any other in the Bible, further attests to their balanced relationship.[40]

Since the lovers are identified with the natural world, this sense of reciprocity extends naturally to the whole garden. In the garden, no one creature has authority over any other. There is no trace of patriarchy or hierarchy. There is no indication that the plants and animals need a governor or that nature is a repository of resources to be managed by people.[41] The stewardship model of relationship between people and earth, portrayed in the first garden stories in Genesis, is absent in the Song.[42]

The Critique of Ownership

Solomon is a complex figure in the Bible; both celebrated and criticized. The biblical story recounts Solomon as a youth, renowned for his wisdom about trees and hyssop, birds, and creeping things (I Kings 5:13). But over time, the royal life ruins him. He constructs a grand home for himself; amasses vast riches, including gold, silver, ivory, and apes; collects exotic horses; acquires 700 wives and 300 concubines; and chases after other gods.[43] While he himself does not lose his kingdom, his heirs will (I Kings 11:9-12). In the Song too, the profligate Solomon owns extensive vineyards, has an entourage of bodyguards, rides in an extravagant palanquin, and benefits greatly from those who rent out his lands. The ra'yah's belittling name for him is "*ba'al hamon,*" which literally means "master" or "owner of wealth" (Song 8:11). His is a tragic tale of the corrupting influence of wealth and power.

In the Song, both Solomon and the daughters of Jerusalem act as foils to the *ra'yah*. In contrast to Solomon, the *ra'yah* rejects the wealth, ostentation, and gossip of the court. She prefers a leafy bower to a gilded bedroom. She treasures that which money cannot buy: namely, her own garden (8:14). All that she possesses are the gifts of the garden that bedeck her doorway (7:14). All she saves are the choicest fruits for the moment of love's consummation.

To the daughters of Jerusalem, the *ra'yah* is as an outsider; a peasant girl shepherding the sheep and tending the vineyards. Beautiful, independent, and with dark, sunburnt skin, the ra'yah is a threat to the pale-complexioned ladies of the court, and the cruel guards in the streets. The daughters of Jerusalem are initially haughty and proud: they stare down at her (1:6), and the guards, who "protect" the city and its societal norms, beat her (5:7).

The Song closes with an ode to the folly of material grasping. Here the *ra'yah* speaks the most eloquent lines of the Song, "Love is as strong as death.... Were a man to give all the wealth of his house for love, he would be despised" (8:6-7). Love cannot be bought. To conceive of love in terms of money is to make a mockery of love. The tendency toward possession is antithetical to love, to life, and to freedom.

In the end, the lover and her beloved pursue their own destinies; she affectionately sends him off to the mountain of spices (8:14). She dispossesses him and as she does, she frees him, and she frees herself. The lovers' lives oscillate like the cycles of nature. There are times for coming together and times for being apart.

In her very existence, without asserting any moral message, the *ra'yah* is a subversive figure.[44] She asserts that love and freedom will not be found in the accumulation of wealth or the possession of a lover. Love comes with a sense of intimacy with the whole natural world, and freedom comes with trust in life's unfolding.

The Path of Simplicity

The *ra'yah*'s tale is a tale of justice and ethics. Justice flows when people, attuned to nature's cycles, live simply within nature's limits, when everyone has the opportunity to enjoy the common wealth.

The Song models a path of simplicity. The term *simplicity* must not be confused with the word *simplistic*. Living simply is a way of life that helps heal and sustain our earthy home, as it heals us. Living simply implies developing a strong sense of place, of inhabiting the place in which we live—exploring and educating ourselves about its habitats and inhabitants—and protecting that place. It involves making conscious decisions about the interests we pursue, the food we eat, the work we do, the purchases we make, the vacations we choose.

We don't need to travel to the far reaches of the world, at the earth's expense, when so many treasures await us in our backyards. Even if we live in a densely populated area in the city, the world beckons at every moment. What is that delicate flower rising up in the cracks of the sidewalk; what birds are flying overhead? What wild foods, medicines, and fungi are right under our feet?

Today's dire environmental predicament is rooted in a linear economy that assumes that we can take from the earth without replenishing her gifts. It stems from our distorted relationship to the nature, where a few enjoy a disproportionate measure of the earth's wealth and pour their wastes into the earth's waters, land, and atmosphere in return.

For many, living simply is not so simple, especially if we have allowed ourselves to become beholden to a society that fills the airwaves with subtle messages designed to convince us that our happiness depends on what we own—a society that promises that our desirability and our success are a function of our material possessions.

In the Song, the *ra'yah* knows that the amassing of wealth is a hollow pursuit, because money cannot buy the most precious gift: love. The Song tells a story of nature's abundance and generosity, while illuminating the folly of imagining that life's riches could be secured by acquiring more things.

WHOLINESS

Wholeness is the most basic ecological concept. It means that everything in the universe is connected to everything else. It means that we are all kin. It means that we cannot live without each other—the earth and all her inhabitants.

In English, the word "wholeness" is etymologically related to the word "holiness."

As we know, the ancient sage Akiva called the Song the "holy of holies," yet the holy one is never even mentioned in the Song. The lack of reference to the holy one may be a hint that holiness permeates the Song yet is simply not named. Naming the transcendent could reduce the sanctity, the fullness of life to an abstraction. Judaism after all discourages speaking the proper name for God. How can you contain eternity in a word? How can you capture the breath of all being in language?

This commentary suggests that the holiness of the Song lies in its vision of wholeness; the interconnected, inviolable relationships that underly the health of the whole earth. The Song's gardens—both the woman's garden and the many floral, forested, fruiting, and perfume gardens are integrated whole systems. They can especially be appreciated when compared to the parched landscapes and the barren women whose stories drive many of the Torah's narratives.[45] The most serious threat to life on earth is the inability of land and body to bring forth fruit. The sumptuous floral landscape of the *Song*, promising a world that will flourish, diversify, and blossom forever, is a testament to wholeness.

While the chapter on "Justice" points toward this wholeness, I am suggesting that there is even a more direct connection between wholeness and divine holiness. I refer to this confluence of holiness and wholeness as "wholiness." Three recurrent themes in the Song capture a sense of divine wholiness: the language of presence and being, the attention to scent, and a focus on oneness.

The Experience of Presence

If we are looking for evidence of the divine in the Song, we need to consider some of the ways that God is intuited by the biblical authors. In the Bible, the proper name for God, as indicated by the Hebrew letters, *yud heh vav heh*, is a conjugation of the verb "to be," and can be understood simply as "being," "is-ness," or "presence." In biblical Hebrew, verb forms appear in the past or the future tenses (more correctly understood as the perfect and imperfect tenses). I once heard someone suggest that the fact that verbs are not written in the present is a testament to the idea that the only "present" tense in the Hebrew imagination is God.

The divine presence can be felt as the connective tissue, the vivid aliveness and the sense of "presence" that infuses the Song.

Living consciously in the present and living in the divine presence are connected. The Song invites us into the present through its arresting images, metaphorical language, lack of active verbs, and sensual portraits. The word *hineh*, which occurs several times, is often translated as "Look!" but may be better understood as a gasp. It calls us to stop and sink into the moment to attend to the present.[46] The Song's plants and animals, living in the present—not worrying about the future or the past—create a palpable "presence" in the Song. The vivid floral landscape of shapes, colors, and smells beckon the reader to come to their senses and be present to the body of the world; to smell and look and touch.[47]

The Song hints at the "presence" of God when the *ra'yah* bids the daughters to take an oath in the name of the gazelles and the deer of the field (2:7; 3:5, 8:4). The practice of oath taking involves a brief ceremony with God standing as witness. Yet the Song's thrice repeated ode to wholeness, in which the *ra'yah* begs the daughters of Jerusalem to swear that they will let love unfold in its own time, invokes gazelles and deer as witness. That the Hebrew word *tzva'ot* can refer to gazelles while also suggesting one of God's names, *Adonai tzva'ot*, Lord of hosts, has prompted some scholars to suggest that this association between God and the gazelle is not coincidental here, but rather quite intentional.[48]

The Song beckons us to know the animals and plants and the land viscerally, not just through our minds.[49] The sense of intimacy with the whole world is the path into the divine presence. Although there is a narrative line in the Song, what seems most essential is this embodied experience of the garden of the earth.

Reyach and *Ruach*

Curiously, while hearing and seeing are the dominant senses in the Bible, in the Song, the sense of smell predominates.[50] The Song opens with the taste of wine and kisses, and the fragrance of scented oils, and it closes with a mountain of spices. The atmosphere throughout the Song is redolent with fragrance: perfumed oils, earthy myrrh, intoxicating lily, exotic spices, aromatic mandrake, cedar, and juniper. The air, which we so often characterize as an empty space—as an absence—is a conscious presence in the Song. The intoxicating fragrances of the Song invite the reader into a rich experience of bodies and breath.

The Hebrew word *reyach* ("scent" or "smell"), occurs more in the Song of Songs than anywhere else in the Bible, other than in Exodus and Leviticus where it is paired with the word *nichoach*. There it has a specific meaning: the pleasing smell of the sacrifices. *Reyach nichoach* is the sweet smell of the smoke that rose to the heavens when the priests offered up animals on the altar to God.

In the Song, the word *reyach* is always associated with the fragrant smells of the plants of the natural world or the oils derived from them. The poet seems to intimate that the scent of fragrant oils which infuse the atmosphere of the Song of Songs, suggests a communion with the divine. It was, after all, through the *reyach nichoach*, the pleasing smell of the sacrifices, that ancient peoples communicated with God.

There is another hint of the connection of fragrance, reyach, to a divinity in the Song. *Reyach* shares the same root letters as the Hebrew word *ruach*, which can mean wind, breath, or spirit. In Genesis, God first appears as *ruach Elohim*: the wind of God. There is an essential connection between the divine, the wind, and the diaphanous scent of flowers carried by the wind. The unique pervasiveness of reyach in the Song hints at a confluence of the aromatic atmosphere and the spaciousness of God.[51] In Bible scholar Michael Fishbane's words, "The holy fragrance of being" permeates the Song.[52]

Oneness

The first religious principle a Jewish child learns is that God is *one*. Jews recite the mantra of the *oneness* of God in each of our communal prayers. Each time we pray, we proclaim the words from the Bible: *Sh'ma Yisroel Adonai Eloheinu, Adonai Echad.* "Listen, Israel: The Lord our God is *one*" (Deut 6:4).

While many people assume that this formula is a statement of the uniqueness of God—that there is *only one* God, rather than many gods as ancient Israel's neighbors affirmed—I have always understood the *oneness* of God as a testimony to the inter-relatedness of all being. If God is *one*, and also infinite, that oneness must encompass the whole of creation. And if God is one, then we and all the creatures of the world are related—kin—bound together in the *oneness*.

The Song illuminates the reality of *oneness* more vividly than any other biblical text. *Oneness* bespeaks the creatures (humans included) and habitats knit together. *Oneness* is the integration of scent and spirit. *Oneness* is the sense of woman as land. The *dod*, the male lover, after counting the myriad images of love's beauty, arrives breathless and concludes, "the *whole* of you is beautiful—you have no imperfection" (4:7). It is as if the totality—the allness—the integration of all aspects of woman/land is what is most compelling. Later in another portrait, the *dod* proclaims, "One is she" (6:9). Her own wholeness or oneness points to the oneness of God.

In the Song, the experience of divinity is an experience of the interbeing of all life—an experience of reality as one organic whole with no independent parts. From the *oneness* streams all things, a web of relationships that is both inviolable and in flux like the waters of a river. In the words of indigenous author Kaitlin Curtice, "The bloodline of God is connected to everything."[53]

*

Max Weber wrote in the mid-twentieth century that modernity is characterized by the "disenchantment of the world."[54] The earth, once perceived as alive and enchanted, appears dead or inert to most westerners. Oblivious to the sentience of the natural world, we defile the earth with little consideration for the consequences of our actions. Retrieving a sense of the earth's intrinsic value and its aliveness is fundamental to encouraging an enlightened citizenry that lives and acts responsibly, with the earth in mind.

The Song of Songs captures this sense of aliveness. The Song transmits the Bible's most profound ecological message in poetry, creating a sensual experience of the natural world. Over and over, it likens the lovers to the land and its inhabitants, asserting the indelible connection between humanity and earth. It reimagines the world as garden ecosystem, vibrant and whole and suffused with love. It pictures a land in which praise for the other, be it human or animal creature, plant or the land, is continually on the lips of lovers. It illustrates that beauty derives from the earth and its creatures, and that beauty can both capture the heart and ignite a caring for something beyond oneself. It shuns material striving and possessiveness and intimates that love and justice will flow when all recognize that the health of the whole earth depends on the reciprocal relations among all her inhabitants.

The ancient rabbis imagined the Song as a handle by which they could interpret the Torah.[55] They envisioned the Torah as a cup filled with a precious elixir, but without a handle to hold the cup, no one could drink. What would it mean if we applied the Song's ecological vision to our interpretations of the Hebrew Bible today? What if we were to approach the book that has influenced the lives of so many Jews and Christians for thousands of years with an ecological lens?

An even more radical tenth-century midrash claims that the Song of Songs is equivalent to the Torah itself: "Had Torah not been given, it would have been possible to conduct the world on the basis of the Song of Songs alone."[56] What would it mean if we tried to align our lives with the values of the Song—if we actually approached the Song as the Bible?

Today, we must come together across religious and cultural divides as citizens of this one earth. Biblical traditions have the ability to mobilize millions of people, yet calcified interpretations of the Bible and narrow understandings of the divine have created barriers to more expansive readings of the texts. The Song's deeply ecological perspective and its ability to evoke the sacred through a vocabulary of wholeness, offers a vitally important message for our age.

PART THREE

THE SONG OF SONGS: AN ECOLOGICAL COMMENTARY

NAVIGATING THE SONG OF SONGS

Some people become frustrated in their attempts to understand the Song if they are reading a direct translation of the Hebrew, since the text does not specify characters, nor does it clarify who is speaking to whom or give cues for scene changes or flashbacks. Many words that appear in the Song appear nowhere else in the Bible, and in several instances the Hebrew itself is uncertain. Furthermore, since the Hebrew pronouns can be ambiguous, it can be difficult to discern the subject of a particular verse. Is the poet speaking of the beloved or an apple tree, or both? All of this ambiguity, as well as the Song's profusion of metaphors, can lead to uncertainty in interpretation and a blurring of boundaries between body and land, and between dreams, memories, and present reality. Each commentator must draw their own conclusions based on grammar and context. Much is left to the commentator's intuition and imagination.

The ambiguity of the Song is not a negative assessment.

It leads us into the in-between—the place of the unknown and the place of possibility. The Song is like an impressionistic painting that looks different depending on the angle from which we gaze at it. It can lead people to vastly different and even contradictory readings. The narrative—assuming there is one—meanders and spirals, increasing in intensity, presenting images, and then circling back to revisit some of the same images. Through the impressions and ambiguity, the poet of the Song creates a hazy, dreamy atmosphere.

While the beauty of the Song can be found in its multitude of intertwining meanings, the intention and uniqueness of this commentary is to tease out the threads of the Song's ecological vision. As such, this commentary will not be examining and commenting on the more popular understandings of the Song, nor will it dwell on the romance between the two lovers. The ecological dimension of the Song is powerful, yet so interwoven in the fabric of the text, that it has often gone unnoticed. The goal of this volume is to illuminate the deep ecological intelligence embedded at the heart of the Song.

WHO'S WHO IN THIS COMMENTARY

Given the ambiguity of the text, the commentator must make choices about the identity of the characters and the tone of their voices. I make the following assumptions:

The **shepherd girl** is the central character of the Song. She is called *rayati* by the beloved: "ra'yah" can mean both "friend" and "shepherdess"; the "ti" suffix means "my." The ra'yah knows and appreciates nature's ways and she lives and loves according to nature's cycles. She finds her freedom in a life of simplicity, balance, and proportion. Her wisdom grows and flowers through the Song and becomes explicit with her soliloquy on the nature of love in the final chapter.

The **male beloved** supports the *ra'yah*. She calls him "*dod*," which means "beloved." He honors the *ra'yah*'s natural beauty and shares her values and her appreciation for the glory of nature. Notably, their relationship is reciprocal and whole.

Solomon the King is associated with a place called *Ba'al hamon* (not mentioned elsewhere in the Bible), a name which can mean "master of money" (Song 8:11). His lavish carriage and his profitable vineyards suggest that he has an appetite for the material riches of the world (Song 3:9, 8:11). This view of Solomon is informed by the biblical Solomon, a complex character who is praised for his peaceful reign and construction of the Temple, yet criticized for his enormous harem, vast stable of horses, and grandiose building projects.

The **daughters of Jerusalem** have been associated with the women of Solomon's harem. They initially act like a foil to the ra'yah. They function like a Greek chorus: their singsong chants, interspersed throughout the text, give the reader a break from the suspense of the drama and an opportunity to reflect on the story.

A NOTE ABOUT THIS TRANSLATION

My intention with this translation was to offer a relatively literal rendering with the hopes of illuminating the Song's natural history and ecology, as well as its poetry. I am entirely indebted all those who have translated the Song before me including the Jewish Publication Society, Ariel and Chana Bloch, Yehuda Feliks, and the many rabbis and scholars who wrestled with various verses of the Song. Their word choices often influenced mine.

THE SONG OF SONGS

¹ The Song of Songs for Solomon

COMMENTARY ———————————————————

Traditionalists claim that the Song of Songs was written by King Solomon.

However, like much of the Song, the inscription to Solomon is ambiguous. The final chapter of the Song appears to criticize Solomon's materialism. There, Solomon is associated with a place, mentioned nowhere else in the Bible, called *Ba'al hamon*, which can be translated as "master of money."

Perhaps Solomon—in his older years—is reflecting back on his life as a young man, and the ways in which he was seduced by a life of power and wealth. Kohelet (Ecclesiastes), another biblical book traditionally attributed to Solomon, offers a powerful criticism of materialism as well. Some have suggested that the Song's attribution to Solomon may be ironic.

Deeper meanings may lie in the name Solomon itself. The name *Solomon* shares the same root letters, *sh-l-m* as the Hebrew

¹ שִׁיר הַשִּׁירִים אֲשֶׁר לִשְׁלֹמֹה:

word for peace, *shalom*. The root *sh-l-m* can also mean "wholeness," and it is this sense of the word that grounds this commentary.

Ra'yah   2   Let him kiss me with the kisses of his mouth
for your love is better than wine.

3   Your scented oils are good!
Even your name flows like oil.
For this, the women love you.

COMMENTARY

The Song opens with the female character dreaming of her beloved.
The male character refers to the woman as *rayati*, "my friend" or
"my shepherdess." She calls him *dodi*, "my beloved." This commentary refers to the couple by the names they use for each other, *ra'yah*
and *dod*.

It can be challenging to track the dialogue of the Song since
subject and pronouns can vary from one verse to the next. In a
dream state, in which images waver and shift, such changes would
not be unusual.

The atmosphere is suffused with the *dod*'s, or male beloved's,
fragrance. While all the senses in the Song are heightened, the sense
of smell is especially pronounced. Both characters in the Song are
identified by their scent.

The sense of smell is our most primordial sense. While animals
rely on their sense of smell to identify territory, find mates, and
navigate relations with predators and prey, we modern Westerners

² יִשָּׁקֵנִי מִנְּשִׁיקוֹת פִּיהוּ
כִּי־טוֹבִים דֹּדֶיךָ מִיָּיִן:

³ לְרֵיחַ שְׁמָנֶיךָ טוֹבִים
שֶׁמֶן תּוּרַק שְׁמֶךָ
עַל־כֵּן עֲלָמוֹת אֲהֵבוּךָ:

tend to emphasize sight and hearing, often neglecting smell. It is as if we have a cultural bias against the nose. Yet the nose is responsible for the most essential activity, breathing: it gives us life. The sense of smell subtly influences our behavior, emotions and sensuality. In French, "to have a nose for something" is to have an intuition, to know something is true without physical evidence. Perhaps the Song is inviting readers to open up to their intuition to access the deeper natural wisdom that lays dormant in the text.

Ra'yah   4   Draw me after you; let's run!

The king brought me into his chambers.
We will revel and rejoice in your love;
we will savor it more than wine.

Rightly, they love you.

COMMENTARY ───────────────────────────

Notably, the woman speaks first. Her voice is especially striking since the voice of the feminine is often subdued or absent elsewhere in biblical literature.

With her entreaty, the *ra'yah* pulls us across the threshold into the world of her imagination. She runs with a "king"—not necessarily an actual king, but *her* king—to his chamber, into the innermost recesses. She imagines their delight. His love is intoxicating to everyone.

The use of the pronoun "we" instead of "I" may situate the poem in the public sphere: it is the *ra'yah's* story and it is also a communal story.

Some of the strangeness of the Song can become more understandable when, as Ellen Davis suggests, we recognize that the poet of the Song occasionally lifts verses or phrases from the Bible and slightly amends them to fit the meaning of the Song. Davis notes that "We will revel and rejoice in it" from Psalm 118:24 is likely the

מָשְׁכֵנִי אַחֲרֶיךָ נָּרוּצָה ⁴

הֱבִיאַנִי הַמֶּלֶךְ חֲדָרָיו
נָגִילָה וְנִשְׂמְחָה בָּךְ
נַזְכִּירָה דֹדֶיךָ מִיַּיִן

מֵישָׁרִים אֲהֵבוּךָ:

source text for Song 1:4.[57] The ancient rabbis, for their part, heard echoes of the Torah in the vocabulary of the Song and developed allegorical interpretations to explain them.

Ra'yah   5 I am black and lovely
O daughters of Jerusalem,
like the tents of Kedar,
like the drapes of Solomon.

6 Don't stare at me because I am black,
because the sun gazed at me.
My mother's sons were angry with me.
They made me guard the vineyards
but my own vineyard, I did not guard.

COMMENTARY

The *ra'yah* emerges from her fantasy and responds to the daughters
of Jerusalem who look askance at her. She is proud of her dark skin.
She is not like the other young women whose pale complexions are
a reflection of lives lived inside the court.

The *ra'yah* is strong, independent and capable, engaged in what
is often considered man's work: tending the vineyards and shepherding the sheep. Her skin is blackened, like the prized hides of
the black-haired goats used for the Bedouin tents. She earned her
rich dark color.

Her burnt skin suggests that it is the height of summer. The
narrative of the Song appears to follow a seasonal arc.

Notably, the *ra'yah*'s brothers are identified as "sons of her
mother." The matriarchal line predominates in the Song. A father
is not named. This feminine dominance stands out in a patriarchal
culture in which leadership and authority is passed on through the
male lineage: through Abraham, Isaac, and Jacob. While the *ra'yah*

⁵ שְׁחוֹרָה אֲנִי וְנָאוָה
בְּנוֹת יְרוּשָׁלָ͏ם
כְּאָהֳלֵי קֵדָר
כִּירִיעוֹת שְׁלֹמֹה:

⁶ אַל־תִּרְאוּנִי שֶׁאֲנִי שְׁחַרְחֹרֶת
שֶׁשֱּׁזָפַתְנִי הַשָּׁמֶשׁ
בְּנֵי אִמִּי נִחֲרוּ־בִי
שָׂמֻנִי נֹטֵרָה אֶת־הַכְּרָמִים
כַּרְמִי שֶׁלִּי לֹא נָטָרְתִּי:

is strong and independent, she is still beholden to her brothers and expected to guard their vineyards.

The vineyard is both an actual garden and a metaphor for the woman's body. The *ra'yah* must guard her brother's vineyard, but as a woman, she has been told that she can't claim ownership either to the garden of her own body, or to their vineyards.

Ra'yah 7 Tell me, love of my soul;
    Where do you graze your sheep?
    Where do you rest them at noon?
    Why should I lose my way
    among the flocks of your friends?

COMMENTARY

The *ra'yah* initiates the first contact with the *dod*; a bold act for a young woman in ancient Israel. She hints at a rendezvous, asking after the whereabouts of his sheep. A shepherdess, as her pet name, *ra'yah*, suggests, she would know that the flocks would roam freely, browsing the grasses on the hillsides in the morning. At noon, they would huddle in the shade of a rock to avoid the heat of the midday sun.

As Ted Hiebert discusses in *The Yahwist's Landscape*, ancient Israel was a mixed agrarian economy.[58] The Israelites would herd their flocks in the desert hills and grow their fruits, vegetables, and grains in the valleys, taking advantage of the land's topography to ensure sufficient food supply all year, regardless of the vagaries of weather.

הַגִּידָה לִּי שֶׁאָהֲבָה נַפְשִׁי ⁷
אֵיכָה תִרְעֶה
אֵיכָה תַּרְבִּיץ בַּצָּהֳרָיִם
שַׁלָּמָה אֶהְיֶה כְּעֹטְיָה
עַל עֶדְרֵי חֲבֵרֶיךָ:

Dod   8   If you do not know, most beautiful of women,
        follow the tracks of the sheep
        and graze your kids
        by the shepherds' tents.

COMMENTARY ————————————————

The *dod,* perhaps playfully, sidesteps the *ra'yah's* questions. She is a shepherdess; she should know where the sheep graze. She should follow the lead of her flock. The animals know the way.

    A pattern of movement emerges throughout the Song. As the *ra'yah* comes near, the *dod* pulls back. When he approaches, she is evasive. Each has their own rhythm, turning toward and away from each other, like the earth as it turns toward and away from the sun.

⁸ אִם־לֹא תֵדְעִי לָךְ הַיָּפָה בַּנָּשִׁים
צְאִי־לָךְ בְּעִקְבֵי הַצֹּאן
וּרְעִי אֶת־גְּדִיֹּתַיִךְ
עַל מִשְׁכְּנוֹת הָרֹעִים:

Dod   9 Like my own mare of Pharaoh's chariots,
            I have imagined you, my friend.
     10 Your cheeks are fine with copper charms,
            a string of beads at your neck.
     11 We will adorn you with golden charms
            and silver balls.

COMMENTARY

Egypt was the one of the wealthiest empires known to Ancient Israel. The mares of the Egyptian king, or Pharaoh, bedecked with jewels, would have been among the most stunning creatures imaginable. The *dod* envisions the *ra'yah* like the Pharaoh's mares: strong, independent, and wild, adorned with gold and silver pendants to accentuate her cheeks and neck. He promises her more jewels to enhance her natural beauty.

⁹ לְסֻסָתִי בְּרִכְבֵי פַרְעֹה
דִּמִּיתִיךְ רַעְיָתִי:
¹⁰ נָאווּ לְחָיַיִךְ בַּתֹּרִים
צַוָּארֵךְ בַּחֲרוּזִים:
¹¹ תּוֹרֵי זָהָב נַעֲשֶׂה־לָּךְ
עִם נְקֻדּוֹת הַכָּסֶף:

Ra'yah 	¹² While the king lay beside me
my nard wafted its scent.
¹³ A pouch of myrrh is my love to me
lodged between my breasts.
¹⁴ A cluster of henna blooms is my love to me
in the vineyards of Ein Gedi.

COMMENTARY

The *ra'yah* dreams of another night with her king. She has oiled her body with the rare aromatic nard, and wears a small pouch filled with the crystallized resin of myrrh. The nard, or spikenard, was a precious perfume; an essential oil made from the roots of a plant in the honeysuckle family imported from the Himalayas. Myrrh is a perfume made from a thorny tree species, Commiphora. The *ra'yah* is transported by the fragrance. She imagines her beloved as an infusion of this earthy smelling myrrh and rose-scented henna.

The *ra'yah* imagines a tryst in Ein Gedi, or perhaps she is reminded of Ein Gedi by the sprigs of henna and the myrrh in her spice pouch. Ein Gedi is a fertile oasis fed by perennial springs at the foot of a mountain in the midst of a desert. It provides a water source for the diverse local plants and animals as well as the hundreds of migrating species that pass through. Ein Gedi was well-known for the henna that grew in its fields. The two words "*Ein*"

¹² עַד־שֶׁהַמֶּלֶךְ בִּמְסִבּוֹ
נִרְדִּי נָתַן רֵיחוֹ
¹³ צְרוֹר הַמֹּר דּוֹדִי לִי
בֵּין שָׁדַי יָלִין:
¹⁴ אֶשְׁכֹּל הַכֹּפֶר דּוֹדִי לִי
בְּכַרְמֵי עֵין גֶּדִי:

and "*Gedi*" mean respectively "spring" and "goat-kid," and are emblematic of the natural world in the Song.

Dod   ¹⁵ You are beautiful, my friend;
       You are beautiful,
       your eyes are doves.

Ra'yah   ¹⁶ You are beautiful, my beloved,
       fine indeed.
       Yes! Our leafy bed is fresh and green;
      ¹⁷ the beams of our house are cedar,
       our rafters are junipers.

COMMENTARY

The word for beauty, *yafah,* rarely used in the Bible occurs repeatedly in the Song and is central to its meaning. The lovers continually refer to each other's beauty in terms of the plants and animals, with whom they live in intimate relation. The emphasis on beauty is detailed in four portraits of the lovers beginning with Song 4:1.

The *ra'yah* delights in planning their forest abode. Their leafy nest will feel and smell like the aromatic woods. She values the fragrance of cedar and the protection that the cedar offers. The sweet-smelling and airy retreat is a testament to the intimacy with nature and the integration of person and place that the *ra'yah* espouses.

¹⁵ הִנָּךְ יָפָה רַעְיָתִי
הִנָּךְ יָפָה
עֵינַיִךְ יוֹנִים:

¹⁶ הִנְּךָ יָפֶה דוֹדִי
אַף נָעִים
אַף־עַרְשֵׂנוּ רַעֲנָנָה
¹⁷ קֹרוֹת בָּתֵּינוּ אֲרָזִים
רחיטנו בְּרוֹתִים:

2

Ra'yah ¹ I am a lily of Sharon,
a lily of the valley.

Dod ² Like a lily among the brambles
so is my friend among the young women.

Ra'yah ³ Like an apple among the trees of the woods,
so is my beloved among the young men.

In his shade, I delighted, and sat
and his fruit was sweet in my mouth.

COMMENTARY

The *ra'yah* sees her lover and herself as the flora of her world. She had already likened him to myrrh and henna. Now she is a lily, alluring and sweet-smelling. Her satiny petals invite touch and connection. The *dod* playfully extends her metaphor: He compares his lily to the other women of Jerusalem, who are like brambles—twisted and barbed.

The *ra'yah* quickens the game. She likens the *dod* to an apple tree whose fruits are sweet and delicious, not like other trees—including evergreens, for example, whose cones are dry and inedible.

In verse 3, the *ra'yah* sits blissfully in "his"—or "its"—shade, savoring the taste of "his"—or "its"—apples. The Hebrew possessive form could refer either to the tree or to the man. The Song is intentionally ambiguous, melding man and tree.

The apple tree is the Song's signature tree. While "apple" is the common translation of the Hebrew word, *tapuach*, in verse 3, "orange" and "apricot" have also been suggested. *Tapuach* may

¹ אֲנִי חֲבַצֶּלֶת הַשָּׁרוֹן
שׁוֹשַׁנַּת הָעֲמָקִים:

² כְּשׁוֹשַׁנָּה בֵּין הַחוֹחִים
כֵּן רַעְיָתִי בֵּין הַבָּנוֹת:

³ כְּתַפּוּחַ בַּעֲצֵי הַיַּעַר
כֵּן דּוֹדִי בֵּין הַבָּנִים

בְּצִלּוֹ חִמַּדְתִּי וְיָשַׁבְתִּי
וּפִרְיוֹ מָתוֹק לְחִכִּי:

come from the root, *n-ph-ch,* which means "to blow" or "to scent," or from *t-ph-ch,* which means "to swell" or "become round." Both root meanings give a fuller picture of the scented and sensual apple tree.

Before the seventeenth century, the English word "apple" was a generic term referring to most fruits. This commentary continues the tradition of translating *tapuach* as "apple" in light of its original meaning. The use of "apple" also hints at a connection between the Song and the Garden of Eden, where the unnamed forbidden fruit was often assumed to be an apple.

Ra'yah 4 He brought me to the banquet hall,
his flag over me was love.

5 Sustain me with raisins,
heal me with apples
for I am sick with love.

6 His left arm under my head
and his right arm embraced me.

COMMENTARY ——————————————————————

The *ra'yah* imagines her *dod* becoming bolder. He brings her out in public to proclaim his love to the world.

The *ra'yah* is overcome with love sickness. Her fantasies are too much. She begs for raisins to revive her. She longs for apples—perhaps a reference to their fragrant scent or to her *dod*, whom she associates with the apple tree—to heal her.

She imagines herself wrapped in his arms, and is soothed. Verse 6 is a refrain that repeats through the Song. It grounds the Song in a circle of love.

⁴ הֱבִיאַנִי אֶל־בֵּית הַיַּיִן
וְדִגְלוֹ עָלַי אַהֲבָה:

⁵ סַמְּכוּנִי בָּאֲשִׁישׁוֹת
רַפְּדוּנִי בַּתַּפּוּחִים
כִּי־חוֹלַת אַהֲבָה אָנִי:

⁶ שְׂמֹאלוֹ תַּחַת לְרֹאשִׁי
וִימִינוֹ תְּחַבְּקֵנִי:

Ra'yah   7   Swear to me, daughters of Jerusalem,
       by the gazelles and the deer of the field.
       Do not awake or arouse love
       until it pleases.

COMMENTARY

This is the first of three refrains that punctuate the Song. The *ra'yah* begs the daughters to refrain from intruding on love's path. Any efforts to arouse love prematurely could squelch it. She knows that the time has not arrived for the flowering of love. Love has its own internal clock, its own gestation period. Just like plants and animals, love will blossom and bear fruit in its own time. The *ra'yah*'s relationship to the seasons of love is a central theme of the Song.

The *ra'yah* asks the daughters to take an oath by the gazelles and the deer. In ancient Israel, oaths were sworn with God as witness; however, in the Song, the animals stand as witness. They embody the divine. The Hebrew names of these two animals even *sound* like two Hebrew names for God: The Hebrew for gazelles, *tzva'ot* is an unusual plural form that brings to mind the more common divine epithet *Adonai tzvaot*, or "Lord of hosts." The phrase "deer of the field," *ayalot hasadeh*, has similar consonants to another name for God, *El shaddai.*

7 הִשְׁבַּעְתִּי אֶתְכֶם בְּנוֹת יְרוּשָׁלַם
בִּצְבָאוֹת אוֹ בְּאַיְלוֹת הַשָּׂדֶה
אִם־תָּעִירוּ וְאִם־תְּעוֹרְרוּ אֶת־הָאַהֲבָה
עַד שֶׁתֶּחְפָּץ:

In intimating the godliness of the gazelles and deer, the poet of the Song expresses an ecological vision that honors the divinity of all the creatures.

Ra'yah   8   The sound of my beloved!
Here! He is coming:
leaping over mountains,
sprinting over hills.
     9   My love is like a gazelle or young stag.
There! He is standing behind our wall:
gazing through the windows,
peering through the lattice.

COMMENTARY

Yehudah Feliks suggests that the tale of the lovers is simultaneously a tale of two gazelles. He imagines that the human players morph into their spirit animals and back again. He proposes that when the *ra'yah* speaks the words "gazelle" and "deer" (verse 7), the *dod* recognizes the vibration of her voice from afar, and transforms into his alter identity, the gazelle.

Aroused by hormones and the intensity of desire, the young *dod* leaps over mountains and sprints over hills. It is early spring, the mating period for ancient Israel's gazelles. Following his female's pheromone track, the gazelle-like dod abandons his characteristic sense of caution and wanders into human enclaves to find his mate.[59] Gazelles, it should be noted, once mated, remain monogamous for the rest of their lives. (Feliks notes that while some gazelle species mate in the fall, these gazelles mate in spring).[60]

While Feliks's reading may seem radical to some, his suggestion bears reflection. The ancient rabbis would stretch their

⁸ קוֹל דּוֹדִי
הִנֵּה־זֶה בָּא
מְדַלֵּג עַל־הֶהָרִים
מְקַפֵּץ עַל־הַגְּבָעוֹת:
⁹ דּוֹמֶה דוֹדִי לִצְבִי אוֹ לְעֹפֶר הָאַיָּלִים
הִנֵּה־זֶה עוֹמֵד אַחַר כָּתְלֵנוּ
מַשְׁגִּיחַ מִן־הַחַלֹּנוֹת
מֵצִיץ מִן־הַחֲרַכִּים:

imaginations as they interpreted the biblical passages. Original interpretations were welcomed. New readings could speak truth for future generations, even if they seemed marginal when they were written.

Ra'yah   ¹⁰ My love called to me and said,

Dod   Get up, my friend, my beauty,
and come away.
¹¹ For now the winter is past,
the rain is over and gone.
¹² The scarlet blossoms have appeared in the land,
the time of the songbird has come,
the voice of the turtledove is heard in our land.
¹³ The green figs form on the fig tree,
the flowering vines give off their fragrance.
Get up my friend, my beauty,
and come away.

¹⁴ My dove in the cranny of the rocks,
in the secret places of the cliff,
Let me see your face,
let me hear your voice,
for your voice is sweet
and your face is lovely.

COMMENTARY

When the *dod* finds his mate, he calls to her from outside her wall, beckoning her to get up. The winter rains are over. Scarlet anemones, tulips and poppies dot the landscape and songbirds and turtledoves tweet their songs.[61] Fig tree and grapevine sweeten the air. The world is a riot of color, sound and smell, heralding the arrival of spring.

The *dod* entreats the *ra'yah* to come with him on the spring migration. It is time to seize the energy of spring and join with the other creatures.

¹⁰ עָנָה דוֹדִי וְאָמַר לִי

קוּמִי לָךְ רַעְיָתִי יָפָתִי
וּלְכִי־לָךְ:
¹¹ כִּי־הִנֵּה הַסְּתָו עָבָר
הַגֶּשֶׁם חָלַף הָלַךְ לוֹ:
¹² הַנִּצָּנִים נִרְאוּ בָאָרֶץ
עֵת הַזָּמִיר הִגִּיעַ
וְקוֹל הַתּוֹר נִשְׁמַע בְּאַרְצֵנוּ:
¹³ הַתְּאֵנָה חָנְטָה פַגֶּיהָ
וְהַגְּפָנִים סְמָדַר נָתְנוּ רֵיחַ
קוּמִי לְכִי רַעְיָתִי יָפָתִי
וּלְכִי־לָךְ:

¹⁴ יוֹנָתִי בְּחַגְוֵי הַסֶּלַע
בְּסֵתֶר הַמַּדְרֵגָה
הַרְאִינִי אֶת־מַרְאַיִךְ
הַשְׁמִיעִינִי אֶת־קוֹלֵךְ
כִּי־קוֹלֵךְ עָרֵב
וּמַרְאֵיךְ נָאוֶה:

But now the *ra'yah* is evasive, hiding. She is like a dove, apprehensive and secretive. The *dod* begs her to reveal herself.

Ra'yah ¹⁵ Catch for us jackals,
     the little jackals
     that ruin our vineyards
     when the vines are in blossom.

COMMENTARY ———————————————————————

How could the *ra'yah* abandon her vineyard at a time when the jackals threaten to destroy the new growth? Perhaps she is preoccupied with her own tender grapes or perhaps she is being coy and elusive. Maybe she is calibrated to a different rhythm than the *dod*.

¹⁵ אֶחֱזוּ־לָנוּ שׁוּעָלִים
שׁוּעָלִים קְטַנִּים
מְחַבְּלִים כְּרָמִים
וּכְרָמֵינוּ סְמָדַר:

Ra'yah   ¹⁶ My beloved is mine
                and I am his
                who browses among the lilies.

           ¹⁷ Before the day breathes
                and the shadows flee;
                Turn, my beloved—
                Be like a gazelle or young stag—
                on the craggy mountain.

COMMENTARY ————————————————————

While the *ra'yah* cannot accompany the *dod* just yet, she is commit-
ted to him. She pledges her fidelity. It is a matter of timing, and the
time is not right.

   She reminds him of his gazelle nature. He thrives in the mountains where he can run free in the fresh, cool air. She sends him off
to return to his northern den. He must leave before day breaks or
be exposed and vulnerable to a host of foes and predators, be they
animal or human.

   Just as each season has its own characteristics (weather and
daylength) that elicit particular behaviors of animals and plants,
so too, do day and night. Night affords rest and provides cover for
the lovers to meet safely; it is the time for mystical encounters.
Daytime is for worldly activities. The lovers avoid daylight for fear
of exposure.

16 דּוֹדִי לִי
וַאֲנִי לוֹ
הָרֹעֶה בַּשּׁוֹשַׁנִּים:

17 עַד שֶׁיָּפוּחַ הַיּוֹם
וְנָסוּ הַצְּלָלִים
סֹב דְּמֵה־לְךָ דוֹדִי
לִצְבִי אוֹ לְעֹפֶר הָאַיָּלִים
עַל־הָרֵי בָתֶר:

Ra'yah

1 On my bed in the night,
   I searched for the one I love.
   I searched for him but did not find him.
2 I must get up and go round the city,
   through the streets and the squares,
   I must search for the one I love.
   I searched for him but did not find him.

3 The guards found me
   as they rounded the city.
   Have you seen the one I love?

4 I had barely passed them
   when I found the one I love.
   I held him and would not let him go
   until I brought him to my mother's house,
   to the room of her who conceived me.

COMMENTARY

The *ra'yah* roams the streets, frantically searching for her beloved, whom she has just sent away. She begs the city guards to help. Finally she finds him and she won't let him leave.

Perhaps this scene occurs in real time or perhaps the *ra'yah* is having an anxiety dream. The *ra'yah* recognizes what her beloved means to her once she thinks she has lost him. She regrets sending him off. The Song is a song of yearning; of reaching but not quite touching. This theme repeats throughout.

At the end of the scene above, the *ra'yah* takes her beloved to the place where she was conceived—to her mother's house. Like

3

עַל־מִשְׁכָּבִי בַּלֵּילוֹת ¹
בִּקַּשְׁתִּי אֵת שֶׁאָהֲבָה נַפְשִׁי
בִּקַּשְׁתִּיו וְלֹא מְצָאתִיו:
אָקוּמָה נָּא וַאֲסוֹבְבָה בָעִיר ²
בַּשְּׁוָקִים וּבָרְחֹבוֹת
אֲבַקְשָׁה אֵת שֶׁאָהֲבָה נַפְשִׁי
בִּקַּשְׁתִּיו וְלֹא מְצָאתִיו:

מְצָאוּנִי הַשֹּׁמְרִים ³
הַסֹּבְבִים בָּעִיר
אֵת שֶׁאָהֲבָה נַפְשִׁי רְאִיתֶם:

כִּמְעַט שֶׁעָבַרְתִּי מֵהֶם ⁴
עַד שֶׁמָּצָאתִי אֵת שֶׁאָהֲבָה נַפְשִׁי
אֲחַזְתִּיו וְלֹא אַרְפֶּנּוּ
עַד־שֶׁהֲבֵיאתִיו אֶל־בֵּית אִמִּי
וְאֶל־חֶדֶר הוֹרָתִי:

salmon, who return upstream to their birthing grounds to breed, the *ra'yah* instinctively leads her *dod* to the place of her own birth.

It is noteworthy that a mother is invoked here, as she is repeatedly in the Song, with no mention of a father, highlighting the centrality of the feminine in the Song.

Ra'yah   5   Swear to me, daughters of Jerusalem,
         by the gazelles and the deer of the field,
         Do not awake or arouse love
         until it pleases.

COMMENTARY

The refrain "Swear to me, O daughters of Jerusalem," repeated through the Song, speaks to the importance of timing. Although the *ra'yah* is eager to find her beloved, she begs the daughters of Jerusalem not to interfere with their courtship ritual or to incite love prematurely. The *ra'yah*, attentive to the seasonal cycle of the plants and animals, knows there is also a season for love. She is confident that love will unfold organically in its own time.

⁵ הִשְׁבַּ֣עְתִּי אֶתְכֶ֞ם בְּנ֤וֹת יְרוּשָׁלִַ֙ם
בִּצְבָא֔וֹת א֖וֹ בְּאַיְל֣וֹת הַשָּׂדֶ֑ה
אִם־תָּעִ֧ירוּ ׀ וְֽאִם־תְּעֽוֹרְר֛וּ אֶת־הָאַהֲבָ֖ה
עַ֥ד שֶׁתֶּחְפָּֽץ׃

Daughters 6 Who is she, coming up from the desert
like a column of smoke,
more fragrant with myrrh and frankincense
than all the powders of the spice trader?

COMMENTARY

Another scene. It seems that the daughters of Jerusalem have warmed up to the *ra'yah*. She has revealed her vulnerability—her fear of losing her beloved—and now the women regard her differently than they did in the opening scene when they stared at her. They are mesmerized by her: she is like an apparition coming up from the desert.

Throughout the Song, the *ra'yah* is associated with frankincense and myrrh. Here, she appears diaphanous, weightless as a wisp of smoke, recognizable only by her scent.

The fragrant column of smoke is also suggestive of the Temple since frankincense was reserved for use at the Temple. Hints of the Temple are woven throughout the text pointing to the Song's allegorical meaning.

⁶ מִי זֹאת עֹלָה מִן־הַמִּדְבָּר
כְּתִימֲרוֹת עָשָׁן
מְקֻטֶּרֶת מוֹר וּלְבוֹנָה
מִכֹּל אַבְקַת רוֹכֵל:

Ra'yah 7 See the bed of Solomon.
Sixty warriors encircle it,
from the warriors of Israel.

8 All carrying swords,
skilled in warfare.
Each, his sword on his thigh,
against the terror of night.

9 King Solomon made for himself a palanquin
from the cedars of Lebanon.

10 Its pillars, he made of silver,
its back of gold,
its seat of purple linen.
It was laid out in love
by the daughters of Jerusalem.

COMMENTARY

This section (3:7-11) has confounded scholars. Many assume these verses should be a response to the question, "Who is this?" from 3:6. However, the subject in 3:7 is not a person, but rather some kind of structure with its furnishings (3:9-10).

It is important to remember that the Song is a collage of images and associations. The poem functions like a dream; it makes its own emotional sense and doesn't rely on conventional narrative approaches. Biblical texts are open and porous and invite us to bring our own meaning and readings into them.

Solomon's luxurious coach is made from resources extracted from far-off places—cedars of Lebanon, pillars of silver, cushions of gold—and he has an army to protect his bed. Solomon's weightiness is juxtaposed to the weightlessness of the *ra'yah*—she is column of smoke. While Solomon made this structure *for himself* (verse 9), the *ra'yah* owns nothing other than her garden and the fragrances of myrrh and frankincense that waft through the air for all to share.

7 הִנֵּה מִטָּתוֹ שֶׁלִּשְׁלֹמֹה
שִׁשִּׁים גִּבֹּרִים סָבִיב לָהּ
מִגִּבֹּרֵי יִשְׂרָאֵל:

8 כֻּלָּם אֲחֻזֵי חֶרֶב
מְלֻמְּדֵי מִלְחָמָה
אִישׁ חַרְבּוֹ עַל־יְרֵכוֹ
מִפַּחַד בַּלֵּילוֹת:

9 אַפִּרְיוֹן עָשָׂה לוֹ הַמֶּלֶךְ שְׁלֹמֹה
מֵעֲצֵי הַלְּבָנוֹן:

10 עַמּוּדָיו עָשָׂה כֶסֶף
רְפִידָתוֹ זָהָב
מֶרְכָּבוֹ אַרְגָּמָן
תּוֹכוֹ רָצוּף אַהֲבָה
מִבְּנוֹת יְרוּשָׁלָם:

This whole section can be understood as ironical. It may appear that the author is awed by this palanquin and this display of wealth, but the Song's chapter 8 suggests that the poet of the Song is critical of Solomon's extravagance, as were other biblical authors.

Ra'yah   ¹¹ Go out and see, daughters of Zion,
King Solomon,
with the crown that his mother crowned him
on the day of his wedding,
on the day of his heart's delight.

COMMENTARY ─────────────────────────

In verse 7, the *ra'yah* had encouraged the daughters to observe Solomon the king, and perhaps to question the person they have long admired. She reminds them that it was his mother—not his father—who crowned and empowered him as king.

¹¹ צְאֶינָה וּרְאֶינָה בְּנוֹת צִיּוֹן
בַּמֶּלֶךְ שְׁלֹמֹה
בָּעֲטָרָה שֶׁעִטְּרָה־לּוֹ אִמּוֹ
בְּיוֹם חֲתֻנָּתוֹ
וּבְיוֹם שִׂמְחַת לִבּוֹ:

4

Dod

¹ How beautiful you are, my friend, how beautiful!
Your eyes are doves behind your braids.
Your hair is like a flock of goats
sweeping down Mt Gilead.

² Your teeth are like a flock of ewes
climbing up from the washing pool,
all of them twinned and none of them lacking.

³ Your lips are like a crimson ribbon,
your voice is lovely.
Like a cleaved pomegranate are your cheeks
behind your braids.

⁴ Like the tower of David is your neck
built with turrets,
a thousand shields hang on it,
all shields of warriors.

⁵ Your two breasts are like two fawns,
twin gazelles grazing in the lilies.

COMMENTARY ──────────────────────────────

This passage is the first of four portraits—a genre of descriptive
poetry known as a *waṣf* in Arabic literature—of the lovers. Each
portrait opens and closes with a proclamation of the lover's beauty,
and in between, each lover paints a picture of the other. Notably,
the lovers interpret each other's beauty in terms of the plants and
animals of the landscape that they love.

The *dod* begins his portrayal by describing the *ra'yah*'s facial
features and works his way down her body. He likens her to the
flora and fauna, native to the land of Israel. The curve of her eyes,

4

הִנָּךְ יָפָה רַעְיָתִי [1]

הִנָּךְ יָפָה

עֵינַיִךְ יוֹנִים מִבַּעַד לְצַמָּתֵךְ

שַׂעְרֵךְ כְּעֵדֶר הָעִזִּים

שֶׁגָּלְשׁוּ מֵהַר גִּלְעָד:

שִׁנַּיִךְ כְּעֵדֶר הַקְּצוּבוֹת [2]

שֶׁעָלוּ מִן־הָרַחְצָה

שֶׁכֻּלָּם מַתְאִימוֹת וְשַׁכֻּלָה אֵין בָּהֶם:

כְּחוּט הַשָּׁנִי שִׂפְתוֹתַיִךְ [3]

וּמִדְבָּרֵיךְ נָאוֶה

כְּפֶלַח הָרִמּוֹן רַקָּתֵךְ

מִבַּעַד לְצַמָּתֵךְ:

כְּמִגְדַּל דָּוִיד צַוָּארֵךְ [4]

בָּנוּי לְתַלְפִּיּוֹת

אֶלֶף הַמָּגֵן תָּלוּי עָלָיו

כֹּל שִׁלְטֵי הַגִּבּוֹרִים:

שְׁנֵי שָׁדַיִךְ כִּשְׁנֵי עֳפָרִים [5]

תְּאוֹמֵי צְבִיָּה הָרוֹעִים בַּשּׁוֹשַׁנִּים:

partially veiled by her braids, suggests a dove hiding in the crevice of a rock. Her wavy hair recalls a herd of goats gamboling down the mountain. Her teeth are pearly white, like sheep, freshly shorn and bathed, and each tooth and its twin is accounted for. A full complement of teeth was an exceptional mark of beauty in ancient times.

Her lips are red and inviting, her voice resonant, her temples rosy like a pomegranate split open. Her neck is statuesque like the Tower of David, and, like David, she is formidable. Glimmering charms dangle from her necklace, reminiscent of warriors' shields.

Dod   ⁶   Until the day breathes
and the shadows flee,
I will get myself to the mountain of myrrh
and the hill of frankincense.

⁷ The whole of you is beautiful, my friend;
You have no imperfection.

COMMENTARY ───────────────

The *dod* interrupts his playful litany to remind them that daytime is
approaching and he must return to his home in the fragrant mountains (verse 8). Alternatively, he must attend to the *ra'yah*'s own fragrant and shapely mountains—or both.

The Song's poetry invites diverse interpretations. The *ra'yah*
has already been identified with myrrh and frankincense. While
these fragrances are associated with both the hills of the woman's
body and the mountains of the land, they are also reminders of the
holy mountain in Jerusalem, where frankincense and myrrh were
used in the Temple ritual. The identification of these scents with the
Temple is evocative of the presence of the divine.

The *dod* concludes his litany of admiration with the exclamation that the entirety of the *ra'yah* is beautiful. The whole of her
being—implying as well, the whole of the land—is completely
beautiful.

⁶ עַד שֶׁיָּפוּחַ הַיּוֹם
וְנָסוּ הַצְּלָלִים
אֵלֶךְ לִי אֶל־הַר הַמּוֹר
וְאֶל־גִּבְעַת הַלְּבוֹנָה:

⁷ כֻּלָּךְ יָפָה רַעְיָתִי
וּמוּם אֵין בָּךְ:

Dod   8   With me, from Lebanon, my bride;
            Come down with me from Lebanon.
            Journey from the peak of Amana,
            from the peak of Senir and Hermon,
            from the lions' den,
            from the mountains of leopards.

COMMENTARY

The *dod* calls again to his beloved to entice her to join him on the spring migration. He has made this journey before. He refers to each mountain by name—each one is beloved and significant.

He appeals to her sense of the wild and her desire for freedom. He tantalizes her with a vivid description of his place in the mountains in the north of Israel, the life-giving habitat of the wild creatures with whom he shares a home.

8 אִתִּי מִלְּבָנוֹן כַּלָּה
אִתִּי מִלְּבָנוֹן תָּבוֹאִי
תָּשׁוּרִי מֵרֹאשׁ אֲמָנָה
מֵרֹאשׁ שְׂנִיר וְחֶרְמוֹן
מִמְּעֹנוֹת אֲרָיוֹת
מֵהַרְרֵי נְמֵרִים:

Dod   9 You have ravished my heart
        my sister, my bride.
        You have ravished my heart
        with one glance from your eyes,
        with one charm of your necklace.
     10 How beautiful is your love,
        my sister, my bride.
        How much better your love than wine
        and your scented oils better than all the spices.
     11 Nectar drips from your lips, my bride.
        Honey and milk are under your tongue
        and the scent of your dress
        is like the scent of Lebanon.

COMMENTARY

The *dod* reminds the *ra'yah* of their kinship. She is more than a bride to him; she is like a sister. Their relationship is whole and integrated. They are indelibly connected, entwined in an invisible web of relations. Their passion is enduring—not the kind that will burn out by morning.

The *ra'yah*'s scent again figures prominently. She tastes and smells of the intoxicating perfumes of the land, of date honey and goat milk. The *dod* recognizes the *ra'yah* as a daughter of Israel—the land of milk and honey. The Hebrew word for scent, *reyach*, closely connected to the word *ruach*, meaning "air" or "wind," hints at the *ra'yah*'s and the land's intimate relation with the divine, *ruach Elohim*, the Bible's first name for God. The *ra'yah*'s mouth is a doorway to the land, the source of life.

The word Lebanon has a whole constellation of meanings that point to various facets of the Song and its many interpretations. Lebanon is the home of the cedars, the most majestic trees of the

9 לִבַּבְתִּנִי
אֲחֹתִי כַלָּה
לִבַּבְתִּינִי
בְּאַחַד מֵעֵינַיִךְ בְּאַחַד עֲנָק מִצַּוְּרֹנָיִךְ:
10 מַה־יָּפוּ דֹדַיִךְ
אֲחֹתִי כַלָּה
מַה־טֹּבוּ דֹדַיִךְ מִיַּיִן
וְרֵיחַ שְׁמָנַיִךְ
מִכָּל־בְּשָׂמִים:
11 נֹפֶת תִּטֹּפְנָה שִׂפְתוֹתַיִךְ כַּלָּה
דְּבַשׁ וְחָלָב תַּחַת לְשׁוֹנֵךְ
וְרֵיחַ שַׂלְמֹתַיִךְ
כְּרֵיחַ לְבָנוֹן:

ancient Near East, the same trees Solomon chose to construct
the Temple in Jerusalem. The cedars were also treasured for their
enduring fresh and spicy aroma. The word *Lebanon* shares the same
consonants with the Hebrew *levanah*, which means frankincense,
the spice used to anoint the structures of the Temple. Lebanon
and Jerusalem must have been indelibly linked in the minds of the
ancient Israelites. Levanah also refers to the moon and the color
white, the color of both the moon and frankincense sap. The Song
conveys all of these intertwining layers, revealing a deep and complex web of connections to the land and the natural world.

¹² A locked garden is my sister, my bride,
a locked well,
a sealed spring.

¹³ Your branches are an orchard of pomegranates
with the choicest fruits,
henna with nard
¹⁴ nard and saffron, calamus and cinnamon,
with all the frankincense trees,
myrrh and aloes,
with all the finest spices.

¹⁵ A spring in the garden,
a well of living waters
that stream from Lebanon.

COMMENTARY

The *dod* catalogues all of the *ra'yah*'s complex aromas: she is a bouquet of every plant yielding scent, every spice and herb. The *dod* finds her/its fragrances especially enticing. Even the tree bark is valued for its incense

To the *dod*, the *ra'yah* is a garden paradise, reserved but not yet ready for her lover. In the mythic imagination, she is the Garden of Eden, and she is the Tree of Life in the midst of the garden bearing every fruit and herb. Both the psalmist and Ezekiel associated Jerusalem and the Temple with the Garden of Eden, the place where the river of life originates.[62]

While water is often scarce in the land of Israel, it flows freely in Eden, and the sumptuous garden is lush and green. Ecologically speaking, gardens represent fertility and wholeness. They speak to life's continual flowering and possibility.

The *ra'yah* can be understood here as woman, as the Garden of

¹² גַּן נָעוּל אֲחֹתִי כַלָּה
גַּל נָעוּל
מַעְיָן חָתוּם

¹³ שְׁלָחַיִךְ פַּרְדֵּס רִמּוֹנִים
עִם פְּרִי מְגָדִים
כְּפָרִים עִם־נְרָדִים:
¹⁴ נֵרְדְּ וְכַרְכֹּם קָנֶה וְקִנָּמוֹן
עִם כָּל־עֲצֵי לְבוֹנָה
מֹר וַאֲהָלוֹת
עִם כָּל־רָאשֵׁי בְשָׂמִים:

¹⁵ מַעְיַן גַּנִּים
בְּאֵר מַיִם חַיִּים
וְנֹזְלִים מִן־לְבָנוֹן:

Eden, as the Tree of Life and as the Temple: all sources of life in the
Israelite imagination.

Rayah   ¹⁶ Awake, north wind!
Come, O south!
Blow upon my garden.
Let its spices flow out;
Let my beloved come to his garden
and eat its choicest fruits.

COMMENTARY ————————————————————————

The *ra'yah* calls out to the winds from two of the four cardinal directions. In mystical Jewish literature, the winds are associated with the four directions. The wind is the circulatory system of the earth, the courier of all air-borne messages: from pheromones to speech to weather to seeds. The *ra'yah* entreats the wind to carry her tree-sweet scents to her beloved, that he may come and partake of his garden.

עוּרִי צָפוֹן ¹⁶
וּבוֹאִי תֵימָן
הָפִיחִי גַנִּי
יִזְּלוּ בְשָׂמָיו
יָבֹא דוֹדִי לְגַנּוֹ
וְיֹאכַל פְּרִי מְגָדָיו:

5

Dod   ¹ I have come to my garden,
     my sister, my bride,
     I have gathered my myrrh with my balsam,
     I have eaten my honeycomb with my honey,
     I have drunk my wine with my milk.

     Feast, friends; Drink!
     Be drunk with love!

COMMENTARY

The wind blows the fragrances of the *ra'yah*'s garden to the dod. He partakes of all the sensual delights—the scents and tastes. The poet may be assuming a literal garden or imagining the *ra'yah* as a garden—or both.

The *ra'yah* is again identified with honey, wine, and milk. The common moniker for Israel, the land of milk and honey, refers to Israel's mixed agrarian economy of herding and agriculture. Milk points to the centrality of goats in ancient Israel, and honey to the date palm tree. The *ra'yah* is continually identified with the land and its fruits.

The *dod* is so eager for a taste that he doesn't waste time trying to extract the honey from the honeycomb. He dives in whole-heartedly and shares his delight and the abundance of the garden with all of his friends.

Many readers of the Song suggest that the lovers consummate their love at this juncture, since here, the *dod* appears to enter the

1 בָּאתִי לְגַנִּי
אֲחֹתִי כַלָּה
אָרִיתִי מוֹרִי עִם־בְּשָׂמִי
אָכַלְתִּי יַעְרִי עִם־דִּבְשִׁי
שָׁתִיתִי יֵינִי עִם־חֲלָבִי

אִכְלוּ רֵעִים שְׁתוּ
וְשִׁכְרוּ דּוֹדִים:

garden, and friends seem to be gathered at a celebration—perhaps a wedding. However, the Song is poetry and much of it is a dream-scape, so it is difficult to make definitive assertions. The subsequent verses suggest that the time has not yet arrived for love's fruition. In this commentary, where the arc of the seasons is taken as central to the Song's meaning, I suggest that love's consummation occurs later in spring, at the time of the wheat harvest and the first fruits.

Ra'yah   2   I was asleep
but my heart was awake.
The sound of my beloved—knocking.

Dod   Open to me my sister,
my friend, my dove, my perfect one,
for my head is drenched with dew,
my hair with the mist of the night.

COMMENTARY

In another night time scene, the *ra'yah* is in her bed on the verge of sleep when the *dod* appears at her door, eager to enter.

He calls her "sister," "dove," and "friend." His relationship to her is full and integrated. He is ready for an intimate encounter.

² אֲנִי יְשֵׁנָה
וְלִבִּי עֵר
קוֹל דּוֹדִי דוֹפֵק

פִּתְחִי־לִי אֲחֹתִי
רַעְיָתִי יוֹנָתִי תַמָּתִי
שֶׁרֹאשִׁי נִמְלָא־טָל
קְוֻצּוֹתַי רְסִיסֵי לָיְלָה:

Ra'yah 3 I had taken off my robe,
Am I to dress again?
I had washed my feet,
Am I to soil them?

4 My beloved reached his hand for the latch,
my insides were trembling for him.

5 I rose up to open for my beloved,
my hands oozing myrrh,
my fingers dripping myrrh
on the handle of the lock.

6 I opened for my beloved,
but my love had turned and gone.
My soul left with his word.

I searched for him but did not find him.
I called to him, but he didn't answer me.

7 They found me—
the guards that circle the city.
They struck me and hurt me;
they stripped me of my veil—
those guards of the walls.

COMMENTARY

The *ra'yah*, however, holds back. She has undressed for bed, and now she hesitates. By the time she decides to pull herself out of bed and open the door, it is too late. He is gone, and she is desolate.

This scene highlights the pattern of approach and retreat that characterizes the lovers' relationship. Early on it seemed to be a game, but now the *ra'yah* sees that the game has consequences.

The *ra'yah* takes to the streets looking for her beloved, crying out for him. The city guards assume she is crazy or a harlot,

³ פָּשַׁטְתִּי אֶת־כֻּתָּנְתִּי
אֵיכָכָה אֶלְבָּשֶׁנָּה
רָחַצְתִּי אֶת־רַגְלַי
אֵיכָכָה אֲטַנְּפֵם:

⁴ דּוֹדִי שָׁלַח יָדוֹ מִן־הַחֹר
וּמֵעַי הָמוּ עָלָיו:

⁵ קַמְתִּי אֲנִי לִפְתֹּחַ לְדוֹדִי
וְיָדַי נָטְפוּ־מוֹר
וְאֶצְבְּעֹתַי מוֹר עֹבֵר
עַל כַּפּוֹת הַמַּנְעוּל:

⁶ פָּתַחְתִּי אֲנִי לְדוֹדִי
וְדוֹדִי חָמַק עָבָר
נַפְשִׁי יָצְאָה בְדַבְּרוֹ

בִּקַּשְׁתִּיהוּ וְלֹא מְצָאתִיהוּ
קְרָאתִיו וְלֹא עָנָנִי:

⁷ מְצָאֻנִי הַשֹּׁמְרִים
הַסֹּבְבִים בָּעִיר
הִכּוּנִי פְצָעוּנִי
נָשְׂאוּ אֶת־רְדִידִי מֵעָלַי
שֹׁמְרֵי הַחֹמוֹת:

wandering the streets alone at night. They perceive her as a threat
and respond aggressively.

Ra'yah   8   Swear to me, daughters of Jerusalem,
If you find my beloved,
Tell him
I am sick with love.

Daughters   9   How is your beloved better than another lover,
most beautiful of women?
How is your beloved better than another
that you adjure us so?

COMMENTARY

The *ra'yah* is beginning to recognize the gravity of love. Earlier she had begged the daughters to stay away—to leave love alone and let it gestate in its own time. Now, she is so bereft that she implores the young women to help her.

8 הִשְׁבַּעְתִּי אֶתְכֶם בְּנוֹת יְרוּשָׁלָם
אִם־תִּמְצְאוּ אֶת־דּוֹדִי
מַה־תַּגִּידוּ לוֹ
שֶׁחוֹלַת אַהֲבָה אָנִי:

9 מַה־דּוֹדֵךְ מִדּוֹד
הַיָּפָה בַּנָּשִׁים
מַה־דּוֹדֵךְ מִדּוֹד
שֶׁכָּכָה הִשְׁבַּעְתָּנוּ:

Ra'yah

¹⁰ My beloved is dazzling and ruddy,
celebrated among ten thousand.

¹¹ His head is like the finest gold;
his locks are curled,
black as a raven.

¹² His eyes are like doves
besides a water channel,
bathed in milk,
set in fulness.

¹³ His cheeks are like a bed of spices,
a treasure of perfumes.
His lips are lilies,
oozing, dripping myrrh.

¹⁴ His arms are cylinders of gold
set with jasper.
His belly is smooth ivory
studded with sapphire.

¹⁵ His thighs are columns of marble
founded in sockets of gold.
Majestic as Mount Lebanon,
A young man like a cedar!

¹⁶ His mouth is sweet.
All of him is delightful.
This is my beloved and this is my friend,
O daughters of Jerusalem.

COMMENTARY

Just as the *dod* admired every facet of the *ra'yah*'s body, now she marvels at him. She begins at his head and travels south, praising him. It is as if she is touring the landscape of Israel, taking note of its flora, fauna and precious stones. His face and hair recall raven and dove, gardens and lilies. His scent is intoxicating like myrrh,

דּוֹדִי צַח וְאָדוֹם 10
דָּגוּל מֵרְבָבָה:

רֹאשׁוֹ כֶּתֶם פָּז 11
קְוֻצּוֹתָיו תַּלְתַּלִּים
שְׁחֹרוֹת כָּעוֹרֵב:

עֵינָיו כְּיוֹנִים 12
עַל־אֲפִיקֵי מָיִם
רֹחֲצוֹת בֶּחָלָב
יֹשְׁבוֹת עַל־מִלֵּאת:

לְחָיָו כַּעֲרוּגַת הַבֹּשֶׂם 13
מִגְדְּלוֹת מֶרְקָחִים
שִׂפְתוֹתָיו שׁוֹשַׁנִּים
נֹטְפוֹת מוֹר עֹבֵר:

יָדָיו גְּלִילֵי זָהָב 14
מְמֻלָּאִים בַּתַּרְשִׁישׁ
מֵעָיו עֶשֶׁת שֵׁן
מְעֻלֶּפֶת סַפִּירִים:

שׁוֹקָיו עַמּוּדֵי שֵׁשׁ 15
מְיֻסָּדִים עַל־אַדְנֵי־פָז
מַרְאֵהוּ כַּלְּבָנוֹן
בָּחוּר כָּאֲרָזִים:

חִכּוֹ מַמְתַקִּים 16
וְכֻלּוֹ מַחֲמַדִּים
זֶה דוֹדִי וְזֶה רֵעִי
בְּנוֹת יְרוּשָׁלָ͏ִם:

his legs molded of marble, his torso is ivory. His hands and belly are set with jasper and sapphire, two gemstones of the breastplate of the Temple priests.

He is both lover and friend, a kindred spirit.

6

Daughters   1   Where has your beloved gone,
most beautiful of women?
Where has he turned?
We will seek him with you.

Ra'yah   2   My beloved went down to his garden,
to the spice gardens,
to browse in the gardens
and gather lilies.

3   I am my beloved's
and my beloved is mine.
He who browses among the lilies.

COMMENTARY ———————————————————————

The daughters of Jerusalem, eager to help the *ra'yah*, ask after the *dod*'s whereabouts.

The *ra'yah* responds that the *dod* is content, grazing in the spice gardens (perhaps in Ein Gedi, renowned for its fragrant plants). Some read this passage more sexually and interpret the spice gardens as the garden of *ra'yah*'s own fragrant body.

The *ra'yah* affirms that she and her beloved belong to each other. The words, "I am my beloved's and my beloved is mine" speak to their communion. Theirs is a balanced, mutually beneficial love. And because both the *dod* and the *ra'yah* are embedded in the natural world, their sense of reciprocity extends to the whole of nature.

6

אָנָה הָלַךְ דּוֹדֵךְ
הַיָּפָה בַּנָּשִׁים
אָנָה פָּנָה דוֹדֵךְ
וּנְבַקְשֶׁנּוּ עִמָּךְ:

דּוֹדִי יָרַד לְגַנּוֹ
לַעֲרוּגוֹת הַבֹּשֶׂם
לִרְעוֹת בַּגַּנִּים
וְלִלְקֹט שׁוֹשַׁנִּים:

אֲנִי לְדוֹדִי
וְדוֹדִי לִי
הָרֹעֶה בַּשּׁוֹשַׁנִּים:

Dod

4 You are beautiful, my friend, like Tirzah;
Majestic as Jerusalem,
awesome as a bannered army.
5 Turn your eyes away from me,
because they overwhelm me.

Your hair is like a flock of goats
sweeping down Mount Gilead.
6 Your teeth like a flock of ewes
climbing up from the washing pool,
all of them twinned and none of them lacking.
7 Like a cleaved pomegranate
are your cheeks behind your braids.

8 There are sixty queens and eighty wives
and maidens without number.
9 One is she, my dove, my perfect one,
One is she to her mother—
She is the choice of her who bore her.
Maidens saw and celebrated her.
Queens and the king's wives praised her.

COMMENTARY

It is as if the *dod* hears and responds to the *ra'yah*'s words. He lavishes
her with praise, embellishing his earlier portrait. She is beautiful like
the flora and fauna of Israel, and she is strong and well-defended like a
bannered army. He compares her to the northern city of Tirzah and the
southern city of Jerusalem, Israel's two capitals at the time when Israel
was divided. (The name "Tirzah" comes from the verb *r-tz-h*, which
means favor, and the name "Jerusalem," containing the root *sh-l-m*,
can mean "peace" or "wholeness.") Ellen Davis suggests that by identi-
fying the *ra'yah* with the rival cities of Tirzah and Jerusalem, the poet is
expressing a desire to knit together the divided Israel as one.[63]

⁴ יָפָה אַתְּ רַעְיָתִי כְּתִרְצָה
נָאוָה כִּירוּשָׁלָם
אֲיֻמָּה כַּנִּדְגָּלוֹת:
⁵ הָסֵבִּי עֵינַיִךְ מִנֶּגְדִּי
שֶׁהֵם הִרְהִיבֻנִי

שַׂעְרֵךְ כְּעֵדֶר הָעִזִּים
שֶׁגָּלְשׁוּ מִן־הַגִּלְעָד:
⁶ שִׁנַּיִךְ כְּעֵדֶר הָרְחֵלִים
שֶׁעָלוּ מִן־הָרַחְצָה
שֶׁכֻּלָּם מַתְאִימוֹת וְשַׁכֻּלָה אֵין בָּהֶם:
⁷ כְּפֶלַח הָרִמּוֹן רַקָּתֵךְ
מִבַּעַד לְצַמָּתֵךְ:

⁸ שִׁשִּׁים הֵמָּה מְלָכוֹת וּשְׁמֹנִים פִּילַגְשִׁים
וַעֲלָמוֹת אֵין מִסְפָּר:
⁹ אַחַת הִיא יוֹנָתִי תַמָּתִי
אַחַת הִיא לְאִמָּהּ
בָּרָה הִיא לְיוֹלַדְתָּהּ
רָאוּהָ בָנוֹת וַיְאַשְּׁרוּהָ
מְלָכוֹת וּפִילַגְשִׁים וַיְהַלְלוּהָ:

The reference to the *ra'yah* as the one of sixty "queens" may be the *dod*'s response to her prior references to him as her "king." Earlier, the *ra'yah* had waxed passionately about the *dod*'s praise-worthiness—he was beloved by *all* the young women. Now the buoyant dod responds even more effusively to the *ra'yah*. All the other women—even queens and the women of the harem who were initially haughty or jealous—admire and extol her.

The reiterated theme of oneness in verse 8—"One is she"—is significant. The *ra'yah* is a perfect whole, like the land and like the Garden of Eden. And she is "one" with the land.

Daughters   10   Who is she that appears like the dawn,
               beautiful as the moon,
               pure as the sun,
               awesome as a bannered army?

Ra'yah   11   I went down to the nut grove
               to see the fresh green by the stream,
               to see if the vines had budded,
               if the pomegranates had flowered.

         12 I did not know
               my soul had set me
               amidst the chariots of Ammi-nadib.

COMMENTARY ————————————————————

This scene is a reprise of 3:6, which also begins with these words: "Who is she?"

The daughters now see the the *ra'yah* as a celestial beauty, even more dazzling than the earthly beauty proclaimed by the *dod*. She is radiant like the sun and the moon, energizing and enlivening all life on earth.

The ancient Israelites depended on the celestial bodies to keep track of time. The rhythm of the year was determined by the earth's cycling around the sun. Holidays were determined by the phases of the moon. The mosaic floors of ancient synagogues, often embellished with the signs of the Zodiac, attested to the importance of the stars and planets in the Israelites' lives.

The *ra'yah* visits the nut garden to check on the ripening of the fruits in anticipation of love's revelation. Both pomegranates and grapes flower in mid to late spring.

Verse 12 has long perplexed scholars. The *ra'yah*'s visit to the

¹⁰ מִי־זֹאת הַנִּשְׁקָפָה כְּמוֹ־שָׁחַר
יָפָה כַּלְּבָנָה
בָּרָה כַּחַמָּה
אֲיֻמָּה כַּנִּדְגָּלוֹת:

¹¹ אֶל־גִּנַּת אֱגוֹז יָרַדְתִּי
לִרְאוֹת בְּאִבֵּי הַנָּחַל
לִרְאוֹת הֲפָרְחָה הַגֶּפֶן
הֵנֵצוּ הָרִמֹּנִים:

¹² לֹא יָדַעְתִּי
נַפְשִׁי שָׂמַתְנִי
מַרְכְּבוֹת עַמִּי־נָדִיב:

garden seems to bring about an altered state of consciousness in which she finds herself in the company of princes (literally *ammi* means "my people," and *nadiv* means "prince"). Or perhaps, she is simply responding to the *dod*'s praises from the last scene in which he compares her to royalty.

7

Dod ¹ Return, return
O Shulamite
Return, return
so we may gaze upon you.

Ra'yah Why would you gaze on the Shulamite
in the dance of the Mahanaiim?

COMMENTARY

The *Shulamite* is another name for the *ra'yah*. The word *Shulamite* is composed of the same primary consonants, *sh-l-m,* as the word *shalom,* which means "peace" or "wholeness." It is related to the word Jerusalem—another hint at the confluence of woman and land.

Mahanaiim literally means "two camps." Ellen Davis has suggested that *Mahaniim* refers to Jerusalem's strategic geographical and political position situated between the Northern and Southern kingdoms of Ancient Israel.[64] Alternately, perhaps *Mahanaiim* is the name of a dance that involves two camps of dancers.

Perhaps the *ra'yah* is responding coyly to the *dod*, "Why watch me as I dance?"

7

[1] שׁוּבִי שׁוּבִי
הַשּׁוּלַמִּית
שׁוּבִי שׁוּבִי
וְנֶחֱזֶה־בָּךְ

מַה־תֶּחֱזוּ בַּשּׁוּלַמִּית
כִּמְחֹלַת הַמַּחֲנָיִם:

Dod   ² How beautiful are your feet in sandals,
      O daughter of nobles.
      The curves of your thighs are like jewels,
      the work of an artist's hands.
   ³ Your navel a round bowl;
      Let it not lack for wine.
      Your belly a mound of wheat
      hedged by lilies.
   ⁴ Your two breasts are like two fawns,
      twins of a gazelle.
   ⁵ Your neck is like a tower of ivory;
      your eyes like pools in the Heshbon
      by the gate of Bat Rabim.
      Your nose is like the tower of Lebanon
      watching out over Damascus.
   ⁶ Upon your head—like a garden;
      The hair on your head—like royal purple—
      the king is caught in the tresses.

COMMENTARY

In this third portrait, the *dod* again proclaims his love and admiration for the *ra'yah*. This time—perhaps in response to her dance—he begins his litany at her feet and travels north to her hair. He imagines her navel as a goblet of wine and her belly as a heap of wheat. Her shape is evocative of two essential fruits of the land of Israel: wheat and grapes.

Her long, smooth neck is statuesque like a tower, symbolizing protection. All creatures require some means of protection to thrive; some animals have exoskeletons or fur while some plants have thorns.

Her nose is prominent, a watchtower established to guard Israel from her northern enemies. This image is less surprising when we

מַה־יָּפוּ פְעָמַיִךְ בַּנְּעָלִים
בַּת־נָדִיב
חַמּוּקֵי יְרֵכַיִךְ כְּמוֹ חֲלָאִים
מַעֲשֵׂה יְדֵי אׇמָּן:
שָׁרְרֵךְ אַגַּן הַסַּהַר
אַל־יֶחְסַר הַמָּזֶג
בִּטְנֵךְ עֲרֵמַת חִטִּים
סוּגָה בַּשּׁוֹשַׁנִּים:
שְׁנֵי שָׁדַיִךְ כִּשְׁנֵי עֳפָרִים
תָּאֳמֵי צְבִיָּה:
צַוָּארֵךְ כְּמִגְדַּל הַשֵּׁן
עֵינַיִךְ בְּרֵכוֹת בְּחֶשְׁבּוֹן
עַל־שַׁעַר בַּת־רַבִּים
אַפֵּךְ כְּמִגְדַּל הַלְּבָנוֹן
צוֹפֶה פְּנֵי דַמָּשֶׂק:
רֹאשֵׁךְ עָלַיִךְ כַּכַּרְמֶל
וְדַלַּת רֹאשֵׁךְ כָּאַרְגָּמָן
מֶלֶךְ אָסוּר בָּרְהָטִים:

consider that the sense of smell, the domain of the nose, is distinguished throughout the Song.

Her purple hair is the color of royalty and the color of the curtains that hung in the Temple. Purple dye was extracted from the shells of the mussels found only along this Mediterranean coastline. It would take 8,000 shells to produce one gram of purple dye. The *ra'yah*'s purple-black hair is indicative of her own natural royalty.

Dod   7   How beautiful you are and how very fine
         O love of delights!
     8   Your stature is like a palm tree
         and your breasts like clusters.
     9   I said, Let me climb into that palm tree,
         let me grasp its branches.
         May your breasts be like grape clusters,
         and the scent of your breath like apples.

Ra'yah   10   And your mouth—most excellent wine
         flowing smoothly to my beloved,
         gliding by the lips of those who sleep.

COMMENTARY

The *ra'yah's* tower-like neck and nose give a sense of her ennobled stature. As the *dod* draws closer, she becomes even more majestic, like a palm tree.

The *dod* imagines the *ra'yah* as a pastiche of all the luscious fruits of the garden: clusters of dates (palm), apples, and grapes. The *dod* is overcome by the *ra'yah's* beauty as he reaches for the words to convey her delights. She is every fruit he can conjure. Or perhaps he is climbing an actual tree and imagining her. Her fruits are round, plump and ready to eat.

Verse 10 is puzzling; scholars are uncertain about the meaning of the Hebrew. Perhaps the *ra'yah* concludes the *dod's* poem for him.

7 מַה־יָּפִית וּמַה־נָּעַמְתְּ
אַהֲבָה בַּתַּעֲנוּגִים:

8 זֹאת קוֹמָתֵךְ דָּמְתָה לְתָמָר
וְשָׁדַיִךְ לְאַשְׁכֹּלוֹת:

9 אָמַרְתִּי אֶעֱלֶה בְתָמָר
אֹחֲזָה בְּסַנְסִנָּיו
וְיִהְיוּ־נָא שָׁדַיִךְ כְּאֶשְׁכְּלוֹת הַגֶּפֶן
וְרֵיחַ אַפֵּךְ כַּתַּפּוּחִים:

10 וְחִכֵּךְ כְּיֵין הַטּוֹב
הוֹלֵךְ לְדוֹדִי לְמֵישָׁרִים
דּוֹבֵב שִׂפְתֵי יְשֵׁנִים:

Ra'yah

¹¹ I am my beloved's
and his desire is for me.

¹² Come my beloved
Let's go out into the field,
let's lie among the henna flowers.

¹³ Let's rise up early and go to the vineyards,
let's see if the grapevine has flowered,
if its blossoms have opened,
if the pomegranates have bloomed.
There I will give you my love.

¹⁴ The mandrakes give off their scent,
and at our doors all the choice fruits,
fresh ones as well as those stored away,
my beloved, that I treasured for you.

COMMENTARY

The *ra'yah* repeats the credo of love's reciprocity (see 6:3). The use of the rare word "his desire," *teshukah,* in verse 11 hints at a connection to the Garden of Eden story. In the Garden of Eden, God warns Adam and Eve, after their trespass, that they will each suffer a curse. For Eve, "her desire/*teshukah* will be for her man, and he will rule over her" (Genesis 3:16).

In the Song, the *ra'yah* is redeemed from the curse of male dominance. The *dod desires her,* and while she also loves him, he does not "rule over her." Through their balanced and reciprocal relationship, the lovers help restore the wholeness of the world. Male and female are equal and as one, just as they were in the Garden of Eden (Genesis 1:27).⁶⁵

The *ra'yah* leads the *dod* into the field to lie amidst the flowers and herbs, to breathe in the perfumes of henna, grape, pomegranate, and mandrake. The unfurling of these blossoms intimates that

¹¹ אֲנִי לְדוֹדִי
וְעָלַי תְּשׁוּקָתוֹ:
¹² לְכָה דוֹדִי
נֵצֵא הַשָּׂדֶה
נָלִינָה בַּכְּפָרִים:
¹³ נַשְׁכִּימָה לַכְּרָמִים
נִרְאֶה אִם פָּרְחָה הַגֶּפֶן
פִּתַּח הַסְּמָדַר
הֵנֵצוּ הָרִמּוֹנִים
שָׁם אֶתֵּן אֶת־דֹּדַי לָךְ:

¹⁴ הַדּוּדָאִים נָתְנוּ־רֵיחַ
וְעַל־פְּתָחֵינוּ כָּל־מְגָדִים
חֲדָשִׁים גַּם־יְשָׁנִים
דּוֹדִי צָפַנְתִּי לָךְ:

the season has arrived for the consummation of love. For the first time, the ra'yah explicitly voices her desire: "I will give you my love."

The mandrakes, *duda'im* in Hebrew, literally "love-fruit"—known as an aphrodisiac in biblical times—are the ultimate sign that now is the time for love's fruition (Genesis 30:16-17). They bloom in late spring at the time of the wheat harvest.[66] The beginning of the wheat harvest is also a sign that the holiday of Shavuot is upon them.

Shavuot is known by its many names as the holiday of the "first fruits," of the wheat offering, and of the giving of the Torah. It is the season of revelation. As the first fruits of the wheat are ready to be harvested, and the Torah of love is ready to be given, so the couple is ready to harvest the fruits of their well-tended love.

8

Ra'yah

¹ If only you were as a brother to me,
sucking the breasts of my mother—
If I found you outside,
I would kiss you
and no-one would despise me.

² I would lead you; I would bring you
to my mother's house—
she taught me—
I would give you spiced wine,
my pomegranate wine.

³ His left hand under my head,
his right arm embraced me.

⁴ Swear to me, daughters of Jerusalem,
Why awake and arouse love
until it pleases?

COMMENTARY

As the *ra'yah* speaks to the *dod*, they are bound in an embrace.
Perhaps this feeling of security awakens memories of her mother
and the wholeness of that relationship. The *ra'yah* longs to be as
close to her beloved as she would to a sibling with whom she shared
special moments, nursing at their mother's breasts. She yearns for
intimacy and wants to express her affection publicly without fear
that others might judge her.

The repeated reference to the mother bears reflection. Just like
the gazelles of the field, and the many creatures that return to their
ancestral breeding ground to give birth, the *ra'yah* feels compelled

8

¹ מִי יִתֶּנְךָ כְּאָח לִי
יוֹנֵק שְׁדֵי אִמִּי
אֶמְצָאֲךָ בַחוּץ
אֶשָּׁקְךָ
גַּם לֹא־יָבוּזוּ לִי:

² אֶנְהָגֲךָ אֲבִיאֲךָ
אֶל־בֵּית אִמִּי
תְּלַמְּדֵנִי
אַשְׁקְךָ מִיַּיִן הָרֶקַח
מֵעֲסִיס רִמֹּנִי:

³ שְׂמֹאלוֹ תַּחַת רֹאשִׁי
וִימִינוֹ תְּחַבְּקֵנִי:

⁴ הִשְׁבַּעְתִּי אֶתְכֶם בְּנוֹת יְרוּשָׁלָ͏ִם
מַה־תָּעִירוּ וּמַה־תְּעֹרְרוּ אֶת־הָאַהֲבָה
עַד שֶׁתֶּחְפָּץ:

to take her *dod* to her birthplace—the fertile ground of her mother's house. The mother is emblematic of generativity and the possibility of new life.

The *ra'yah* reiterates her appeal to the daughters, only this time, she questions why anyone would interfere with love's unfolding. The *ra'yah* and her beloved are attuned to the trajectory of love through its seasons, just like the gazelles.

Daughters 5 Who is she rising from the desert,
leaning on her beloved?

Ra'yah   Under the apple tree I awakened you,
There your mother conceived you.
There she bore you.

COMMENTARY

This verse is an echo of the words, "Who is she?" in 3:6. However, in 3:6, the *ra'yah* was identified as a scented and ephemeral column of smoke. Now she is completely embodied, leaning on her beloved in public—something that she had only just dreamed of (8:1).

In the Song, the apple tree is associated with the mother's house. The apple tree is both the place of conception and the place of birth. The couple returns to the apple tree to consummate their own love, as their mothers did for generations before them. According to *Exodus Rabbah* 1:1, the enslaved Israelite women would go out to the fields to give birth under the apple trees.

מִי זֹאת עֹלָה מִן־הַמִּדְבָּר ⁵
מִתְרַפֶּקֶת עַל־דּוֹדָהּ

תַּחַת הַתַּפּוּחַ עוֹרַרְתִּיךָ
שָׁמָּה חִבְּלַתְךָ אִמֶּךָ
שָׁמָּה חִבְּלָה יְלָדַתְךָ:

Ra'yah   6   Set me as a seal upon your heart,
           as a seal upon your arm.
           For love is strong as death,
           jealousy fierce as the grave.
           Its flames are flames of fire,
           a devouring flame.
      7   Great waters cannot
           extinguish love
           and rivers cannot drown it.

           Were a man to give all the wealth of his house for love,
           he would be despised.

COMMENTARY

At the culmination of the Song, the *ra'yah* delivers an exalted soliloquy on the meaning of love. Love animates her life and the life of the world. Love is at the heart of all of the relationships in the Song. It is the energy between the *ra'yah* and the *dod*, and it is the force that binds all creatures together into one inviolable whole. Love is the essence of the Song's "wholiness."

The *ra'yah* entreats the *dod* to engrave their love upon his heart and upon his arm, so as to not forget that love is eternal. The image of "setting a seal on the arm" is evocative of the Jewish prayer, the *V'Ahavta*, "And you shall love," the passage to love God repeated twice daily by observant Jews. The prayer continues, "Bind these words as a sign upon your arm and upon your head." (Traditional Jews enact this commandment by binding tefillin, small leather boxes containing words of Torah on their arms and heads.)

The idea that love could be bought is blasphemous. Love is not

⁶ שִׂימֵנִי כַחוֹתָם עַל־לִבֶּךָ
כַּחוֹתָם עַל־זְרוֹעֶךָ
כִּי־עַזָּה כַמָּוֶת אַהֲבָה
קָשָׁה כִשְׁאוֹל קִנְאָה
רְשָׁפֶיהָ רִשְׁפֵּי אֵשׁ
שַׁלְהֶבֶתְיָה:
⁷ מַיִם רַבִּים לֹא יוּכְלוּ
לְכַבּוֹת אֶת־הָאַהֲבָה
וּנְהָרוֹת לֹא יִשְׁטְפוּהָ

אִם־יִתֵּן אִישׁ אֶת־כָּל־הוֹן בֵּיתוֹ בָּאַהֲבָה
בּוֹז יָבוּזוּ לוֹ:

a kind of merchandise. Love is a gift, given freely, and it must be shared so that all life can flourish.

One wonders if verse 7, "Were a man to give all the wealth of his house for love," is directed at Solomon, whose reputation for extravagance and overindulgence was well known.

Brothers   8   We have a little sister,
and she has no breasts.
What will we do for our sister
on the day that she is spoken for?
9   If she is a wall,
we will build a silver turret upon her,
and if she is a door,
we will enclose her with cedar planks.

Ra'yah   10   I am a wall
and my breasts are like towers,
so I became in his eyes
as one who finds peace.

COMMENTARY

Perhaps the *ra'yah* is recalling a threat from her brothers. She should make herself a "wall," inviolable to all who would attempt to gain access. If she would bar herself off and remain chaste, the brothers would adorn her with silver turrets. But if she would be a "door," open to anyone who wanted to enter, they would sheathe her in cedar wood.

The *ra'yah* is secure and confident. She does not need her brothers' silver turrets; her breasts are adornment and protection enough. She is at peace with herself, assured of her place in her relationships and in the world.

‏אָחוֹת לָנוּ קְטַנָּה
וְשָׁדַיִם אֵין לָהּ
מַה־נַּעֲשֶׂה לַאֲחֹתֵנוּ
בַּיּוֹם שֶׁיְּדֻבַּר־בָּהּ:
אִם־חוֹמָה הִיא
נִבְנֶה עָלֶיהָ טִירַת כָּסֶף
וְאִם־דֶּלֶת הִיא
נָצוּר עָלֶיהָ לוּחַ אָרֶז:

‏אֲנִי חוֹמָה
וְשָׁדַי כַּמִּגְדָּלוֹת
אָז הָיִיתִי בְעֵינָיו
כְּמוֹצְאֵת שָׁלוֹם:

Ra'yah   ¹¹ Solomon had a vineyard
in *Ba'al-hamon*
He gave that vineyard to the guards.
A man would bring for its fruit
one thousand pieces of silver.

¹² My very own vineyard is before me;
Keep your thousand, Solomon!
And two hundred for the guards of the fruit.

COMMENTARY

Solomon's vineyard is in *Ba'al-hamon*, a place never mentioned in the Bible. *Ba'al hamon* can literally be translated as "master of money," and perhaps the Song employs this term to disparage Solomon's unbridled materialism. A *ba'al hamon* can use his money to buy any garden he wants, but he can never buy love (8:7).

Solomon owns and rents out his vineyard to the guards. Each would bring in 1,000 pieces of silver to Solomon and receive 200 pieces in return for their labor. For Solomon, a garden is a commodity. He has no relationship with it; rather he must hire laborers to work the fields and cultivate the fruits.

The *ra'yah* does not need Solomon's property or his wealth. Her body is her garden; and the lush garden of the Song is her home to enjoy and share.

¹¹ כֶּרֶם הָיָה לִשְׁלֹמֹה
בְּבַעַל הָמוֹן
נָתַן אֶת־הַכֶּרֶם לַנֹּטְרִים
אִישׁ יָבִא בְּפִרְיוֹ
אֶלֶף כָּסֶף׃

¹² כַּרְמִי שֶׁלִּי לְפָנָי
הָאֶלֶף לְךָ שְׁלֹמֹה
וּמָאתַיִם לְנֹטְרִים אֶת־פִּרְיוֹ׃

Dod   ¹³ You who dwell in the garden,
         Our friends are listening for your voice.
         Let me hear it!

Ra'yah   ¹⁴ Flee my beloved!
         Be like a gazelle or young stag
         on the mountain of spices.

COMMENTARY ———————————————————————

"You who are sitting in the gardens" refers to the *ra'yah* who is continually identified with gardens. Her friends are eager to hear her voice, to gather the fruits of her embodied wisdom.

The Song ends as the *ra'yah* sends her beloved off at dawn once more. She is secure in their relationship and at ease with their cycles of togetherness and a-part-ness. The *ra'yah* does not need to possess the *dod* to know that their love is real. She trusts in the "wholiness" of the world. She encourages the *dod* to follow his animal nature, wherever it will lead him.

¹³ הַיּוֹשֶׁבֶת בַּגַּנִּים
חֲבֵרִים מַקְשִׁיבִים לְקוֹלֵךְ
הַשְׁמִיעִנִי:

¹⁴ בְּרַח דּוֹדִי
וּדְמֵה־לְךָ לִצְבִי אוֹ לְעֹפֶר הָאַיָּלִים
עַל הָרֵי בְשָׂמִים:

ENDNOTES

[1] What is the "voice of a turtle," I always wondered? The answer—I learned decades later—hinges on the recognition that the Hebrew *tor*, as well as the Old English "turtle," which is derived from the Latin *turtur*, are both onomatopoeic words representing verbal attempts to imitate the cooing call of a dove. The King James translators, working in the 17th century, used the archaic "turtle" rather than the modern English "turtledove," perhaps to emphasize the antiquity of the original text. For the last century, most English translations of the Song of Songs have translated tor as "turtledove," not "turtle", although in 1914 the Jewish Publication Society followed the King James version..

[2] Daniel Grossberg, "Nature, Humanity and Love in Song of Songs" (*Interpretation*, 2005), 59:229-244.

[3] Chana and Ariel Bloch, *The Song of Songs* (Berkeley, CA: University of California Berkeley Press,1995), 32.

[4] Yehuda Feliks, *Song of Songs: Nature Epic and Allegory* (Jerusalem: The Israel Society for Biblical Research, 1983).

[5] Nalungiaq, "Magic Words," *Songs and Stories of the Netsilik Eskimos*, edited by Edward Field (Boston, MA: HMH Books, 1998). According to Jerome Rothenberg, the song was first written down by Danish explorer Knud Rasmussen, who was part Inuit and spoke the Inuit language. During his expedition across arctic America, the Fifth Thule Expedition (1921–1924), he lived with the Netsilik people.

[6] An author of several books on the environmental crisis and the winner of the Blue Planet Prize, Gus Speth is the cofounder of the Natural Resources Defense Council, former dean of the Yale School of Forestry and Environmental Studies founder, founder and former president of the World Resources Institute, and senior advisor to Presidents Jimmy Carter and Bill Clinton. On the Earth Charter podcast Turning Conscience into Action, he discussed "The New Consciousness and the Eightfold Way Towards Sustainability" with Mirien Vilela, Earth Charter International's executive director. Source: earthcharter.org/podcasts/gus-speth/.

[7] This is a historically rare claim, but one that is beginning to grow. While thousands of articles and books have been written on the Song, and several have acknowledged the Song's ecological orientation, only a handful have considered the depth of nature's central role and the inviolable connection between human and nature at the heart of the Song.

Harold Fisch explores the Song's use of metaphor to diminish the distance between human and nature. "There is a kind of imaginative overspill, as the rapture of the lovers overflows into the sphere of geography, transforming the whole land into the object of love," he writes in the book *Poetry with a Purpose: Biblical Poetics and Interpretation* (Bloomington, IN: Indiana University Press, 1988, 92). Fisch concludes that the Song is as much a love poem addressed to a beloved land, as it is a love poem between male and female lovers (Fisch, 98).

Similarly, Francis Landy contends that the Song is as concerned with the relationship between human and nature as it is with that between human beings, and that "exploring the body is equivalent to exploring the world" in his essay, "The Song of Songs," included in *The Literary Guide to the Bible,* edited by Robert Alter and Frank Kermode (Cambridge, MA: Harvard University Press 1987, 306). He writes: "The elaborate combinations of parts of the body and geographic features ... assert the indissolubility of man and the earth..." (Landy, 314).

Biologist Yehuda Feliks, in his highly creative work *Song of Songs: Nature, Epic and Allegory*, reads the Song as a narrative that simultaneously occurs in three realms—that of male and female gazelle, man and woman, and God and Israel (Feliks, 5).

Daniel Grossberg suggests that the Song uses the profusion and potency of nature to convey and illuminate the meaning of love. Love, perceived through nature, he attests, is basic to the design of the universe (Grossberg, 237).

Ellen Davis suggests that the rich natural imagery in the Song can help one to feel God's love for the earth and overcome one's anthropocentric orientation toward the world. "Loving the land is no less essential to our humanity than sexual or religious love," and in fact, it is a religious obligation, she writes in her book *Proverbs, Ecclesiastes and the Song of Songs* (Louisville, KY: Westminster John Knox, 2000, 236).

More recently, Elaine James has explored the landscapes of the *Song* in her book *Landscape of the Song of Songs* (New York: Oxford University Press, 2017), and Rabbi Arthur Waskow has commented on ecological aspects of the Song in his book *Dancing in God's Earthquake* (Maryknoll, NY: Orbis Books, 2020).

[8] The website of Angaangaq Angakkorsuaq, "Uncle," is icewisdom.com.

[9] Clearly, we are not going to encounter modern terms like "environment," "climate," or even "nature" in ancient texts. Our contemporary environmental vocabulary is only about fifty years old. We need to pay attention to the vocabulary that the biblical authors employ to express their ideas and feelings about the natural world, rather than expect to find a modern lexicon or modern conceptions. We also need to judge the text on its own terms—not ours. Furthermore, the Bible tends to reveal its ecological intelligence to those who approach it with curiosity and openness. When people approach the Bible with suspicion, the way that some academics have been trained to read, they may be unable to recognize the more subtle ecological aspects of the text.

[10] Lynne White, "The Historical Roots of the Ecologic Crisis" (*Science*, vol. 155, no. 3767, March 1967, 1203-1207).

[11] The "holy of holies" was the inner sanctum of the traveling tent that accompanied the Israelites through the desert. It contained the holy ark which housed the holy Torah. It was there—in the heart of the community, in the innermost chamber—that God's presence was thought to dwell. Only one time a year, on Yom Kippur, the holiest day of the calendar, would the priest enter into the holy of holies and commune with the Holy Blessed One.

[12] Genesis 1:28-1:31: In these verses, the word *kol* or "everything" is repeated many times. People often assume that the "very goodness" of the sixth day refers to the human creatures who were created on this day, but a close reading of these verses indicates that it is kol or everything all together that is "very good."

[13] Between man and woman (Genesis 3:16), people and land (including its creatures 3:15,17-19) and people and God (3:23), according to Davis (2000, 232) and Michael Fishbane in *The JPS Commentary, Song of Songs* (Lincoln, NE: University of Nebraska Press, 2014, 192-3).

[14] The rabbis associated the holiness of the Song with love. Two Hebrew roots, for "love," "dod" and "ahav," appear repeatedly, in almost half of the Song's 117 verses. Woman and man share an abiding love. The male character is called dod or "beloved." The couple reveal the fullness of their love to each other when the *duda'im*, the love fruit, blooms. The Song's refrain, "Don't wake or arouse love till it pleases," emphasizes the integrity of love. In the final verses, the female character, the ra'yah gives a soliloquy on the meaning of love, the most powerful force in the universe (8:6). While some say that the love in the Song is between a man and a woman, and others say that love is between God and the people, from an ecological perspective, love is the energy that cultivates and nurtures the all the creatures and the web of relationships upon which the earth, God's house, depends. Love is required for the earth to thrive and flourish in perpetuity.

[15] For Humboldt, "the imagination soothed the deep wounds that reason created." In Andrea Wulf, *The Invention of Nature: Alexander Humboldt's New World* (New York: Alfred A Knopf, 2015, 336).

[16] 2:1, 3, 5, 16; 5:13; 6:3; 7:9; 8:5.

[17] 2:9, 2:17, 8:14, 4:5, 7:4.

[18] Feliks, 1983, 56.

[19] Grossberg, 2005, 237.

[20] Fig (2:13), grapes (1:6, 2:15), wheat (7:3), pomegranate (4:3, 6:7, 8:2), date palm (7:7-8), and olive oil (1.3).

[21] Israel is described several times in the Bible as the "land of milk and honey" (Exodus 3:8,17; 13:5, 33:3).

[22] 4:1-4:7, 5:10-5:15, 6:4-6:10, 7:2-7.

[23] Fishbane, 2014, 126-7.

[24] 3:4, 8:2, 8:5.

[25] A.J. Heschel, *The Sabbath* (New York: Farrar, Straus and Giroux, 2005), 2.

[26] Feliks, 1983, 56.

[27] 34, 18.

[28] See Genesis 30:14 for the first mention of mandrakes.

[29] The *omer* period is a 49-day period between Passover and Shavuot when farmers would anxiously await the ripening of their wheat.

[30] Sandra Lubarsky, unpublished manuscript on beauty and sustainability, 2022.

[31] Many Biblical characters were called yafeh or *yafah*/beautiful: Joseph (Gen 39:6); Sarah (Gen 12:11); Rachel (Gen 29:17), Esther (Est 1:11). Sixteen of fifty-one biblical occurrences of yafah show up in the Song.

[32] 1:8, 1:15 (twice); 2:10, 2:13; 4:1 (twice); 4:7; 4:10, 5:9; 6:1, 6:4, 6:10, 7:2, 7:7.

[33] 4:1-7; 6:4-10; 7:2-7; 5:10-16. These portraits of beauty" comprise 27 of the Song's total 117 verses and account for nearly half of the verses in the second half of Song.

[34] The reading of the creatures onto the woman's body has caused Bible scholar Fiona Black to characterize the imagery of Song as "grotesque." (Fiona Black, *The Artifice of Love: Grotesque Bodies and the Song of Songs* (New York: Continuum Books, 2009, 10). Drawing on a cartoon by Den Hart, she imagines a woman with a nose resembling a tower, a mouthful of sheep and a towering neck. Such a hyperliteral reading bespeaks an anthropocentric attitude, that does not grasp the metaphoric power of the natural world and the interconnectedness of woman and land in the Song.

[35] Gerald F. Downing, "Aesthetic Behavior in the Jewish Scriptures: A Preliminary Sketch" (*Journal for the Study of the Old Testament*, 2003) 28.2, 137.

[36] "Anthropocentric (Godlovitch 1994), scenery-obsessed (Saito 1998a), trivial (Callicott 1994), subjective (Thompson 1995), and/or morally vacuous (Andrews 1998)," as noted by Carlson (Allen Carlson, "Environmental Aesthetics" in *The Stanford Encyclopedia of Philosophy*, edited by Edward N. Zalta (Palo Alto, CA: Metaphysics Research Lab, 2016), 4.2.

[37] Carlson, 2016, 3:2.

[38] 2:16, 6:3, 7:11; The word *teshukah*, desire, found only in Song 7:11 and Genesis 3:16 and 4:7 links the two garden stories.

[39] 2:16, 6:3, 7:11.

[40] Davis, 1998, 545.

[41] 1:6, 3:4, 3:11, 6:9, 8:1, 8:2, 8:5.

[42] Genesis 1:28, 2:15.

[43] 1 Kings 10:22, 10:28, 11:3, 11:5-6.

[44] Landy, 2001, 51.

[45] Genesis 12:10, 26:1, 41:54, 43:1, 2 Samuel 21:1, 1 Kings 18:2; Sara (Genesis 11:30), Rebekah (25:21), Rachel (29:31), Hannah (1 Sam1:5), and Manoah's wife (Judges 13:2).

[46] 1:15,16, 2:8, 9, 3:7, 4:1.

[47] The *ra'yah* is called a lily (2:1, 16; 6:3; 7:3) and the *dod*, a flowering apple tree (in contrast to the flowerless trees of the woods), bearing sweet and edible fruits (2.3a).

[48] The claim rests on the similarity in sound (consonants) in the Hebrew between "*tzva'ot*"(gazelle) and God's name, "*Adonai tzva'ot*, and between *ayalot hasadeh*" (deer of the field) and *El shaddai* (another name of God).

[49] Storyteller Kevin Kling has said that "when you are living the five senses you are the most awake that you will ever be."

[50] Sight is also significant, but the sense of smell is unique and unusual.

[51] The pervasiveness of fragrance in the Song also hints at the tabernacle, known for its sweet scent that suggested the presence of God. The scent of the tabernacle emanated from the scented oils used for anointing every object and person that served in the Temple and the incense offering that was burned on the alter at dawn and twilight every day (Exodus 30:7-8, 22-38).

[52] Fishbane, 2014, 126.

[53] Kaitlin Curtice, *Native: Identity, Belonging and Rediscovering God* (Grand Rapids, MI: Brazos Press, 2020), chapter 3.

[54] Max Weber, *Essays in Sociology*, trans. and ed. by H.H. Gerth and C. Wright Mills (New York: Oxford University Press, 1946), 155.

[55] Shir ha Shirim Rabbah 1:8; Yacov Meyer, haaretz.com/jewish/portion-of-the-week/2014-04-17/ty-article/.premium/parashat-song-of-songs-a-handle-for-the-torah/0000017f-e11a-d9aa-afff-f95a0eb80000.

[56] Arthur Green, "I Have Come to My Garden" in *Jewish Review of Books* (Fall 2015): jewishreviewofbooks.com/articles/1874/i-have-come-to-my-garden/.

[57] Davis, 2000, 243.

[58] Theodore Hiebert, *The Yahwist's Landscape* (New York: Oxford University Press, 1996), 75.

[59] Feliks, 1983, 10-16.

[60] In Arabic literature, the gazelle is often associated with the female beauty of the beloved. Linguists theorize that the word ghazal, meaning "love poetry" in Arabic, is related to the word for gazelle. Caliph Abd al-Malik (646-705) was said to have freed a gazelle he had captured because of her resemblance to his beloved.

[61] Feliks, 1983, 29.

[62] Psalm 36:8, Ezekiel 47:1-12.

[63] Davis, 2000, 285.

[64] Davis, 2000, 290.

[65] "Male and female God created them." In Genesis 1:27, man and woman are created simultaneously—perfectly equal. Some of the ancient rabbis considered the first human creature to be a hermaphrodite.

[66] Feliks, 1983, 112.

BIBLIOGRAPHY

Abram, David. 2010. *Becoming Animal*. New York: Vintage Books.

Alter, Robert and Frank Kermode, eds. 1987. *The Literary Guide to the Bible*. Cambridge, MA: Harvard University Press.

Black, Fiona. 2009. *The Artifice of Love: Grotesque Bodies and the Song of Songs*. New York: Continuum Books.

Bloch, Ariel, and Chana Bloch. 1995. *The Song of Songs*. Berkeley, CA: University of California Berkeley Press.

Brennan, Andrew and Yeuk-Sze Lo. "Environmental Ethics." In *The Stanford Encyclopedia of Philosophy* (Fall 2016), edited by Edward N. Zalta. Palo Alto, CA: Metaphysics Research Lab.

Brenner, Athalya and Carole Fontaine, eds. 2000. *The Song of Songs: A Feminist Companion to the Bible*. London: Sheffield Academic Press.

Buber, Martin. 1970. *I and Thou*. New York: Touchstone Books.

Carlson, Allen, "Environmental Aesthetics." In *The Stanford Encyclopedia of Philosophy* (Summer 2016), edited by

Edward N. Zalta. Palo Alto, CA: Metaphysics Research Lab.

Davis, Ellen. 2000. *Proverbs, Ecclesiastes and the Song of Songs.* Louisville, KY: Westminster John Knox Press.

Davis, Ellen. 2003. "Reading the *Song* Iconographically." *Society for Scriptural Reasoning*, vol. 3, no. 2. (jsr.shanti. virginia.edu/back-issues/vol-3-no-2-august-2003-healing-words-the-song-of-songs-and-the-path-of-love/reading-the-song-iconographically/).

Davis, Ellen. 1988. "Romance of the Land in the *Song of Songs*." *Anglican Theological Review* 80:543-546.

Diehm, Christian. 2007. "Identification with Nature; What It Is and Why It Matters." *Ethics and the Environment* 12:1-22.

Dobbs-Allsopp, F.W. 2005. "The Delight and Beauty and Song of Songs 4:1-7." *Interpretation* 59:260-279.

Downing, F. Gerald. 2003. "Aesthetic Behavior in the Jewish Scriptures: A Preliminary Sketch." *Journal for the Study of the Old Testament* 28.2:131-147.

Elliott, Mark. 1994. "Ethics and Aesthetics in the *Song of Songs*." *Tyndale Bulletin* 45.1: 137-152.

Falk, Marsha. 1990. *The Song of Songs.* New York: Pennyroyal Press.

Feliks, Yehuda. 1983. *Song of Songs: Nature Epic and Allegory.* Jerusalem: The Israel Society for Biblical Research.

Fisch, Harold. 1988. *Poetry with a Purpose: Biblical Poetics and Interpretation.* Bloomington, IN: Indiana University Press.

Fishbane, Michael. 2014. *The JPS Commentary, Song of Songs.* Lincoln, NE: University of Nebraska Press.

Fox, Michael. 1985. *The Song of Songs and the Ancient Egyptian Love Songs.* Madison, WI: University of Wisconsin Press.

Goshen-Gottstein, Alon. 2003. "Thinking of/with Scripture: Struggling for the Religious Significance of the *Song of Songs*."*JournalofScripturalReasoning,*vol.3,no.2(jsr.shanti. virginia.edu/back-issues/vol-3-no-2-august-2003-heal- ing-words-the-song-of-songs-and-the-path-of-love/ thinking-ofwith-scripture-struggling-for-the-religious- significance-of-the-song-of-songs/).

Grossberg, Daniel. 2005. "Nature, Humanity and Love in *Song of Songs*." *Interpretation* 59:229-244.

Habel, Norman. 2000. *The Earth Story in Genesis*. Sheffield, UK: Sheffield Academic Press.

Heschel, Abraham Joshua. 2005. *The Sabbath*. New York: Farrar, Straus and Giroux.

Hiebert, Theodore, 1996. *The Yahwist's Landscape*. New York: Oxford University Press.

Jeffers, Robinson. 2002. *The Collected Poetry of Robinson Jeffers*. Edited by Tim Hunt. Palo Alto, CA: Stanford University Press.

Korsmeyer, Carolyn, "Feminist Aesthetics." In *The Stanford Encyclopedia of Philosophy* (Winter 2012). Edited by Edward N. Zalta. Palo Alto, CA: Metaphysics Research Lab (plato.stanford.edu/archives/win2012/entries/ feminism-aesthetics/>).

Lakoff, George, and Mark Johnson. 1980. *Metaphors We Live By*. Chicago: University of Chicago Press.

Landy, Francis. 1987. "The *Song of Songs*." In *The Literary Guide to the Bible,* edited by Robert Alter and Frank Kermode, 305-319. Cambridge, MA: Harvard University Press.

Landy, Francis. 2001. *Beauty and the Enigma*. Sheffield, UK: Sheffield Academic Press.

Leopold, Aldo. 1949. *A Sand County Almanac*. London: Oxford University Press.

Levin, David Michael. 1988. *The Opening of Vision*. New York: Routledge Press.

Lubarsky, Sandra. 2022. Unpublished manuscript on Beauty and Sustainability

Muir, John. 1938/1979. *John of the Mountains: The Unpublished Journals of John Muir*. Edited by Linnie Marsh Wolfe. Madison, WI: University of Wisconsin Press.

Naess, Arne. 1989. *Ecology, Community and Lifestyle: Outline of an Ecosophy*. Translated by David Rothenberg. Cambridge, UK: Cambridge University Press.

Pope, Marvin. 1977. *The Song of Songs*. New York: Doubleday Books.

Rolston, Holmes III. 2002. "From Beauty to Duty" In *Environment and the Arts*, edited by Arnold Berleant, 127-141. Aldershot, UK: Ashgate Publishing.

Scarry, Elaine. 1999. *On Beauty and Being Just*. Princeton, NJ: Princeton University Press.

Segal, Benjamin. 2000. "To Bear, to Teach: The Mother Image in the *Song of Songs*." *Nashim: A Journal of Women's Issues & Gender Studies*, 3:43-55.

Waskow, Arthur. 2020. *Dancing in God's Earthquake*. Maryknoll, NY: Orbis Books.

Weber, Andreas. 2016. *The Biology of Wonder*. British Columbia, Canada: New Society Publishers.

Weber, Max. 1946. *Essays in Sociology*. Translated and edited by H. H. Gerth and C. Wright Mills. New York: Oxford University Press.

Whitman, Walt. 1855. "Song of the Rolling Earth" in *Leaves of Grass. The Walt Whitman Archive*. Gen. ed. Ed Folsom and Kenneth M. Price (whitmanarchive.org).

ACKNOWLEDGMENTS

I first encountered the Song as a young river guide and am grateful to my white-water partner David Wikander for introducing me to rivers and offering me the gift of a deep and abiding relationship with the natural world.

I began to recognize the depth of the Song's ecology two decades ago while studying at Hebrew College, and I wrote a master's thesis exploring its natural wisdom. I am indebted to the many scholars whose reflections on the Song inspired and motivated me—in particular, Yehuda Feliks, Francis Landy, Ellen Davis, and Harold Fisch—and I am grateful to Hebrew College faculty members Natan Margalit and Barry Mesch for their support and guidance, and to the Gann library at Hebrew College.

Thank you to Bible scholar Hilary Marlow for inviting me to contribute an essay to *The Oxford Handbook on the Bible and Ecology* (Oxford University Press, 2022). Several of the ideas in this book first appeared in my essay, "The Ecotheology of the Song of Songs."

Once I realized that my work on the Song needed its own book, I happened to meet Karina Obadia, a French psychologist, through a Zoom connection. I am grateful to Karina for spending many hours *wondering* about the Song with me and translating the lectures of the rabbi and philosopher Marc Alain Ouaknin.

As I began to develop the manuscript, I knew I would need an editor/coach. Thank you to Joel Kaminsky for (re) introducing me to Emily Branton, who pored over every word and had the amazing ability to read my mind and articulate what I could not find words for. Her enthusiasm for the work helped me to believe in myself and bring this project to fruition.

Thank you to Laurie Levy and Steve Altarescu for offering me a quiet place to work in the middle of paradise. Thanks to Ted Hiebert, Doug Anderson, and Rami Shapiro for reading the manuscript and offering feedback; and to Rami for his exuberance, generosity, and introduction to publisher Paul Cohen and Monkfish Book Publishing Company. Thank you to Paul and to editor Susan Piperato and designer Colin Rolfe at Monkfish for their commitment to publishing works on spirituality and ecology, their creativity in producing a magnificent cover that captures the essence of the Song, and their dedication to bringing this book to life. And thank you to Steven Tenenbaum, my spouse, for tracking down great ideas to delight and nourish me, for always *being there,* on-call, to wordsmith, read, and reread—and for giving me the space, an enormous gift, to work.

ABOUT THE AUTHOR

Rabbi Ellen Bernstein is a scholar, environmental thinker, and writer. She began studying religion and ecology in high school; in 1975, she graduated from UC Berkeley's program in Conservation of Natural Resources, one of the first environmental studies programs in the US. In 1988, having taught high school biology and led wilderness river trips for several years, Bernstein founded *Shomrei Adamah*, Keepers of the Earth, the first national Jewish environmental organization, through which she created and hosted the first ecologically-centered Tu B'Sh'vat (Jewish New Year of the Trees) seder and popularized the holiday as a community-wide inter-spiritual ecological arts celebration. In 1990, to commemorate the 20th anniversary of Earth Day, Bernstein organized All Species Parade in Philadelphia, which was witnessed by 10,000 people.

Bernstein's books include *The Trees' Birthday, Let the Earth Teach You Torah, Ecology and the Jewish Spirit, and The Splendor of Creation.* Her most recent book, *The Promise of the Land: A Passover Haggadah,* is the first comprehensive, ecological *haggadah* (guidebook) for Passover.

Bernstein holds an MA in biology and education from Southern Oregon State University, an MA in Jewish studies from Hebrew College, and rabbinic ordination from the Academy of Jewish Religion. She serves on the advisory board for the Yale Forum on Religion and Ecology and Third Act Faith. She lives with her husband Steven Tenenbaum and their dog, Ro'i, in the (aspiring) ecovillage of Mt. Airy in Philadelphia near the Wissahickon Creek, where she hikes most days. To learn more, visit EllenBernstein.org and ThePromiseoftheLand.com.